28/2

# THE
# SUCCESSFUL
# MANAGER

Fenny Bentley

Derbyshire DE6 1LA
Telephone: 01335 350540

WOMEN IN MANAGEMENT
WORKBOOK SERIES

# THE
# SUCCESSFUL
# MANAGER

GERALDINE BOWN · CATHERINE BRADY

*· DOMINO ·*

KOGAN
PAGE

Kogan Page Limited
120 Pentonville Road
London N1 9JN

© The Domino Consultancy

British Library Cataloguing in Publication Data
A CIP record for this book is available from the British Library.

ISBN 0 7494 0518 X

Typeset by BookEns Ltd., Baldock, Herts.
Printed in England by Clays Ltd, St Ives plc.

# Contents

# Preface

Welcome to the second in this series of three books under the title The Women in Management Workbook Series.

*The Successful Manager* assesses the different ways a woman can make a success of her post once she has achieved manager status. It considers the fundamentals of assertiveness and how to think and speak assertively. It looks at communication at work, in terms of both verbal and non-verbal communication. Co-ordinating the activities of staff is a fundamental management process and the book assesses all aspects of managing a team. Finally, it considers how to manage your time in terms of setting priorities and objectives, delegating tasks and how to handle those daily events which seem to rob you of your precious time at work.

The first book in this series, *Are you Ready to Manage?*, was written for women seeking their first management appointment. It assesses skills, qualities and experience and looks at ways of boosting confidence. It also considers the various methods that can be used to find that first appointment, as well as how to settle into a new role.

The third book called *Getting to the Top* considers the steps a woman can take to gain promotion. It looks at breaking down the barriers to advancement, leadership skills and how to get the most out of talks, meetings and interviews. It also provides a practical strategy for dealing with stress and evaluates various tactics for promotion.

The premise of this series is twofold:

- That women in the 1990s are actively seeking management posts of all kinds.

■ That women have the ability to fulfil those posts but sometimes lack the self-confidence and the necessary support to move on and up.

These books will help.

They are designed as a practical guide to management . . . not a series on management theory *and* they are written by women. They contain practical advice on how to get where you want to be. There are ideas and tips which you can apply to your own unique situation and which can be adapted for your own purposes. The books are full of case studies of women already in management positions explaining how certain techniques helped them.

The books are to be read proactively — in other words, to get the most out of them, you have to get involved. So read with a pen in your hand. There are charts and checklists for you to complete — each one taking you further towards your personal management goal!

We wish you every success in your management career.

*Geraldine Bown*
*Managing Director*
*The Domino Consultancy Limited*

## ACKNOWLEDGMENTS

Many people have given their time and expertise in helping us to write this book.

We would like to thank all the women managers who worked with us on this project, providing information for case studies.

We also wish to thank Jan Smith for her cartoons, Zoe Bartells for conducting the research and Ann Baker for editing the series.

# The Women in Management Workbook Series

## The Domino Consultancy Ltd

A series of three self-assessment workbooks devised specifically for women aiming for a career in management. Each workbook deals with a specific stage in a woman's management career using the same 'action learning' approach which allows for a surprising level of self-awareness. Other titles in the series are:

### WORKBOOK 1: ARE YOU READY TO MANAGE?

This, the first book in the series, is for the woman considering a first-time career in management. By assessing her skills and experience the reader is able to draw up a personal profile and an action plan for achieving her ultimate career goal.

ISBN 0 7494 0519 8

### WORKBOOK 3: GETTING TO THE TOP

The final book in the series is for those women who have proved themselves as successful managers but are now focused on joining the ranks of senior management. Topics covered include leadership skills, tactics for promotion, stress management and presentations.

ISBN 0 7494 0517 1

# The Domino Consultancy

The Domino Consultancy Ltd is recognised particularly in the UK and abroad for their expertise in the highly specialised and growing area of women's training and development. They are well known for their high quality training materials and their client base includes NatWest, Midland, Barclays and TSB Banks; Shell UK; the AA; Scottish Homes; PowerGen; Harrods; Manchester Airport; Safeway and Marks and Spencer.

Geraldine Bown is the managing director of Domino, the vice president of the European Women's Management Development Network and representative to the European Women's lobby. She is a frequent speaker at conferences here and abroad.

Catherine Brady is a director of Domino and is responsible for all its development and production projects.

While both being successful business women, the authors each have families and, therefore, firsthand experience of balancing the demands of home and work.

*Introduction*

# Women in Management

At present women make up 45 per cent of the labour force, and the figure will rise to around 50 per cent by the end of the decade. However, sadly, women are still underrepresented in management posts, particularly at middle and senior levels. Perhaps only 4 per cent of these jobs are held by women, and at senior executive level the figure is under 2 per cent.

At junior level the picture is not so gloomy. At the end of the 1980s, women accounted for around 25 per cent of general managerial staff. Women in these roles, however, are still concentrated in traditional 'female' sectors, such as government, the professions, and education and training — and in 'female' occupations such as administration and personnel.

What are the reasons for this? Why has the picture changed so little? The causes are many and varied. Women tend to find the road to the top rocky, compared with their male counterparts. This is particularly so if they have taken time off to rear children. These women find it difficult to compete on equal terms with men when one of the prerequisites for success seems to be accumulating a proven track record in a varied and *continuous* career.

There is also an optimum age for high-flying employees. The early 40s is the age when those who are going to get there have arrived. They have spent their 30s building up skills and experience in preparation for the top jobs. What are women doing at this time of their lives? The majority are rearing their children and therefore lose out on this vital career step. Those who stay the course are more likely to be unmarried or divorced and without children. Family life seems to be a sacrifice some senior women have to make to succeed.

Many companies expect a strong commitment from managers, some of whom work a regular 12-hour day, with travelling and entertaining clients additional burdens. Senior executives are expected to be highly mobile — moving where the company sends them. To turn down the offer of such a move could prove suicidal in career terms — companies do not usually ask twice! Such geographical mobility is fine for a man who is single or has a non-working wife, but the situation is very different for a woman, who is likely to have a partner in a full-time career of his own.

Even when women overcome all these hurdles, they are still faced with what is commonly called the glass ceiling. This is an invisible barrier to success and it often takes a sledgehammer to break through. The glass ceiling means that even if you fulfil all the above criteria, if your face does not fit, forget it. These are the intangible barriers that women come across when applying for posts, particularly if the organisation has always appointed men before. There is almost an inbuilt 'maleness' about many selection processes which women find difficult to penetrate. Employers, up to now, have tended to emphasise the decisive, dominant, and even aggressive side of management at the expense of the cooperative, cohesive and supportive side. In other words, the male over the female side.

The good news is that things are changing. Admittedly, the change is relatively slow, but things are getting better. There are two main reasons for this — economic pressures and changes in the structure of society.

The main economic pressure is the so-called 'demographic time-bomb'. The total number of managers of all types is expected to rise by some 700,000 by the year 2000. At the same time, the number of school-leavers is falling dramatically. The result is that someone will have to fill the void. Companies are gradually realising this and taking steps to rectify the problem. Also, with the creation of the

Single European Market, pressure is on companies to compete. And they can compete successfully only if they have the best — both male and female managers.

Society is also changing for the better, from the point of view of women. The traditional senior manager was often supported by a full-time housewife, but this is less and less frequently the case. More women than ever work and have career aspirations of their own. There are more one-parent families and families in which the woman is the main wage-earner. Women are better educated than before and want to use that education, rather than settle down to a life at home 'in domestic bliss'.

If you are working in management, you may have seen the changes for yourself. Numerous companies are actively encouraging the careers of their women staff, and many company schemes are well publicised. These initiatives include women-only training, enhanced maternity leave and returners' schemes, workplace nurseries and flexible patterns of work.

Thus, things are changing for women in management, and it is a time of great opportunity for those with the will and ambition to succeed. However, women are still in the minority and are likely to remain so for some considerable time. As a result, they tend to face special problems in the workplace — purely and simply because they are women.

This volume focuses on some of the real issues which face all managers today — and women managers in particular. It looks at assertiveness at work and provides some ideas you can try out for yourself. It considers communication — an area where women naturally have a high level of skill. The importance of teamwork is assessed, and there are suggestions on how to build an effective team. There are also some suggestions on how to manage your time — in order that work is not an all-consuming part of your life. Finally, you have the opportunity to draw up an action plan of things you are going to do to help you manage effectively.

There are exercises and self-assessment tests throughout, so read with a pen in your hand.

Enjoy the book and enjoy your career!

# 1
# Assertiveness at Work

In any situation that requires a reaction, there is a choice of responses, both verbal and non-verbal. The outcome of the situation will differ depending on the behaviour adopted. How you handle it will depend on two key elements: firstly, how you regard yourself in relation to the other person or people; secondly, how you feel about yourself. If you lack confidence and have low self-esteem, you will probably feel threatened by the situation and react in one of two ways:

- submissively: keeping a low profile, saying little, feeling concerned and anxious, agreeing as much as you can — and feeling resentful afterwards.
- aggressively: seeing attack as the best form of defence; trying to dominate, getting your point across, not accepting the other person's view, even using sarcasm and personal comments — and probably still feeling resentful.

Both submissive behaviour and aggressive behaviour are characteristic of people who lack confidence, not just in their own abilities but in themselves as individuals.

There is a better way — being assertive.

This chapter considers submissive, aggressive and assertive behaviour and why the last-named is desirable. It provides guidelines on how to think and speak assertively, as well as showing how assertiveness can help in giving criticism.

But first let us define assertiveness.

## WHAT IS ASSERTIVENESS?

Here is a simple definition of assertiveness:

**Getting your needs met without interfering with the rights of others.**

Assertive behaviour means that you express your wants, needs, opinions, feelings and beliefs in a direct and honest way. This involves recognising that in any situation:

- you have needs to be met;
- the other person or persons have needs to be met;
- you have rights;
- the other person or persons have rights;
- the aim is to satisfy the needs and rights of *both* parties.

Here are some examples of the different ways of behaving — aggressive, submissive and assertive. The examples are both verbal and non-verbal — ways of speaking and ways of behaving.

### Ways of speaking

*Aggressive:*

- demanding
- blaming
- threatening
- giving orders inappropriately
- interrupting
- attacking
- putting others down
- forcing others to do things
- expressing opinions as facts
- making assumptions
- using sarcasm

*Submissive:*

- saying 'I'm sorry' often
- saying 'I'm afraid' often
- not getting to the point

- saying 'I should/must/ought' often
- putting yourself down
- not saying what you want/feel/like
- agreeing to things you do not want to do to keep the peace
- backing down
- complaining behind the scenes
- justifying your opinion and yourself

*Assertive:*

- stating clearly what you want/need/feel
- making brief statements that are to the point
- saying 'no' when you want to
- giving praise/constructive criticism when necessary
- finding out the wants/needs/feelings of others
- making decisions
- standing up for yourself
- acknowledging the other person's standpoint
- speaking to people as you wish to be spoken to yourself

## Ways of behaving

|  | Aggressive | Submissive | Assertive |
|---|---|---|---|
| How am I thinking of myself? | superior/ inferior but desperate to hide it | inferior, not as important as everyone else | having equal rights with everyone else |
| How am I feeling? | angry, tense | frightened, anxious, tense | good, calm, excited, feeling of well-being |
| How am I standing? | upright, head in the air, leaning forward or coming close to emphasise points, trying to be physically higher, eg standing when other person is sitting | round-shouldered, head down, chest cramped, turning away from the others, staying at a lower level, eg sitting when others are standing | relaxed, well-balanced, facing the other person directly |

|  | *Aggressive* | *Submissive* | *Assertive* |
|---|---|---|---|
| What are my legs and feet doing? | when standing — feet firmly apart; when sitting — stiffly upright, leaning forward, or foot tapping or swinging; when moving — striding impatiently | shifting weight from one foot to the other, standing with weight on one foot, rolling one foot onto its side, stepping back, shrugging, shuffling | feet about shoulder width apart, weight equally distributed on both feet, standing still |
| What are my hands and arms doing? | hands on hips; fists on hips; arms folded across chest; hand and arm raised as in lecturing; hands clenched tightly; fist thumping; finger pointing, waving or poking; sharp flicks of the wrist; hand-crunching hand-shakes; overhard slaps on the back | hugging the body, wringing hands, covering mouth with hand, nervous fiddling, hands tightly clasped | open hand movements — inviting to speak — arms comfortably by sides, or one hand in pocket, or arms folded loosely; relaxed gestures to emphasise points; when sitting, hands folded comfortably on lap, not fidgeting |
| Where am I looking? | looking down from a height, glaring, staring, hard gaze, narrowing of the eyes, unblinking, looking through or past a person | looking down, looking away, avoiding eye contact, quick furtive glances, eyes darting from side to side when speaking | looking directly at other person at same level, gentle and relaxed look, looking away every so often yet coming back to look at person |
| What is my expression like? | jaw set; teeth clenched; scowling; chin forward; turning red, blue or white with anger; eyebrows | worried, tense, apologetic look; biting lip or inside of cheek; pale or blushing, nervous smiles; | calm; facial muscles and jaw relaxed; firm and pleasant expression; |

|  | Aggressive | Submissive | Assertive |
|---|---|---|---|
|  | raised in dis-belief; indignant, or angry expression; sarcastic grin or sneer | smiling when expressing anger or being criticised | smile when appropriate |
| What is my voice like? | cold, sarcastic, very loud, sharp, threatening, fast, abrupt, clipped | quiet, strained, wobbly, whining, dull or mono-tone, childlike | steady and firm low-pitched, medium volume, clear speech, warm tones |

Notice that the assertive way is the confident way. Confidence and assertiveness are closely linked.

**Assertiveness versus the rest**

Some women managers believe that they need to adopt an aggressive stance to get results. They think that because they are female they have to adopt this approach to compete with men, and that if they do not, their staff will walk all over them. This is particularly true of women who may have behaved submissively in the past and are now determined to show who is boss.

The tactic simply does not work. Aggression will not bring about cooperation, but only alienation. It might bring short-term results, but it certainly will not lay the foundations for long-term success. The people you work with will feel threatened by such behaviour, and the natural thing to do when you feel threatened is to withdraw. Managers who use aggression to get results are also the most isolated.

If you have behaved submissively in the past and now adopt an aggressive stance, one of three things is likely to happen:

■   You will be ignored.
■   You will be laughed at.
■   You will be left alone as people will assume that you are having a brainstorm or that it is the time of the month!

If it is bad to be aggressive, it is just as bad to be submissive. If you behave in this way, it may be just as difficult to gain the full cooperation of your staff because they will not take you seriously. The same applies to your managers. It is good to show willing yourself, but not if it means taking on the workload of others because you do not have the guts to refuse!

What, then, are the benefits of behaving assertively? Why is it the *only* course of behaviour open to good managers?

### Ten good reasons to be assertive

1.  You will feel happier because you will have expressed your needs.

2.  It is more likely that your needs will be met because people will know what they are.

3.  Even if your needs are not met, you will feel better knowing that you handled the situation well and you will have nothing to reproach yourself for.

4.  Your confidence will increase because there will be no situation you will be threatened by.

5.  You will build a better team because you will be able to use everyone's strengths instead of being threatened by them.

6.  You will be able to control your own behaviour and therefore be more effective in negotiating clear and workable agreements.

7.  You will take more initiatives because you will not be as afraid of making mistakes as you used to be.

8.  You will reduce your stress level because negative feelings of anger and frustration will not be allowed to build up.

9.  You will communicate better with people because if you are more direct with others, they are more likely to be direct with you.

10. You will be more comfortable to be around, and thus

your relationships with others will improve at all levels.

While these are certainly good reasons to be assertive, your world will not change magically overnight just because you are using some assertiveness techniques! By controlling your own behaviour, however, your world will certainly be

---

## Case studies

Carol Abbott, Resource Management Project Manager, Derby City Hospital

It's important to be clear about what you are saying and to be able to talk to the other person without inter-ference, to keep eye contact and speak in an even voice, and to be clear and concise. If I think I'm appearing aggressive, then I'll give more non-verbal signals like smiling, or add little sentences; for instance, 'Would you agree?' or 'Do you think?'

In a group it's more difficult, especially if you're not in a position of authority. When talking, I try to ensure that people are quiet, looking at me, and then I give fleeting eye contact to everyone. I use silences to make a point, and I maintain a clear, firm voice.

Senior training adviser, local government

I suppose like most women I've had to learn the techniques. When I really want to achieve something or challenge someone I have to find ways to control my feelings. I have found the scripts you can learn to be particularly useful. For example, I might say 'I realise you may think that, but ——' or 'I feel X, Y, Z about what you have said, and I would like to make the fol-lowing points.'

I just have a couple of little phrases so that when I'm reeling from the impact of something, I can say them quite happily. Some men might call it aggression, so I may perhaps go over it in my head and think, 'Yes, that was OK, you were assertive, not aggressive, and if they think that, then it's their problem not mine.'

improved, even though it might take a while for people around you to see the benefits of your assertiveness.

The case studies opposite reveal what some other women have said on the subject.

Now let us make sure that you can recognise the difference between the three types of behaviour — aggressive, submissive and assertive.

**In the six examples below, a response is given to each of the described situations. Write in the space underneath whether you think the response is *Aggressive, Submissive or Assertive*.**

1.  You do not like people to smoke in your car. After attending a meeting one evening, someone you do not know very well, although she lives near you, asks for a lift and you agree. As you get into the car, she says, 'Oh, where are my matches? I've been dying for a cigarette all evening.'

    RESPONSE:
    'OK. I'll just open my window a bit if you don't mind.'

    **Answer:** ................................................................

2.  You are on an in-service course at which the men are addressed by their first names, and the women are called 'dear'. You find this patronising and irritating. The tutor turns to you and says, 'Well, dear, now what was it you were saying?'

    RESPONSE:
    'I was just saying, baldy, how sick I am of being called "dear".'

    **Answer:** ................................................................

3.  You are engrossed in an urgent piece of work when a member of your department interrupts to ask you to help her with a report she has to write for the following week.

    RESPONSE:
    'I know you need help with your report, but I need

to finish this work. Could I help you with it on Friday?'

**Answer:** ................................................................

4.  You would like to be considered for a senior post which you know is about to fall vacant in the department. You are keen and well qualified to do the job. You decide to see your superior. She asks you to sit down and tell her what is on your mind.

    RESPONSE:
    'I know that Chris is applying for the job and that I've not much chance of getting it . . . but I thought that . . . would it be all right if I put an application in, too?'

    **Answer:** ................................................................

5.  You are asked to collect money to buy a retirement present for a member of staff you do not like.

    RESPONSE:
    'No, I'm not the right person to encourage others to give in this case. I'd like you to ask someone else.'

    **Answer:** ................................................................

6.  You know that there are some training courses which you would very much like to attend. However, the information never seems to get through to you. You go to see your manager.

    RESPONSE:
    'I am keen to improve my performance at work, and I think it is important that I receive training in some areas. Would you let me have a list of the courses run by the training centre so I can discuss with you which are the most suitable for me to attend?'

    **Answer:** ................................................................

Now for some feedback.

|    | ANSWER | COMMENT |
|----|--------|---------|
| 1. | Submissive | Anything-for-a-quiet-life attitude, whether or not your needs and rights are infringed. |
| 2. | Aggressive | Does the tutor realise that his use of 'dear' offends you? Some women do not seem to mind. Making a deliberately offensive remark is not the best way of saying how you feel about his use of language. And if he is using it as a deliberate put-down, your response will encourage him to counter in the same vein. |
| 3. | Assertive | Both of your needs can be met now. |
| 4. | Submissive | Putting yourself down before you start. You are hardly giving the impression that you are promotable. |
| 5. | Assertive | Saying 'no' directly without waffling but giving a reason and making a reasonable suggestion. |
| 6. | Assertive | It would be very difficult to refuse this request. |

The next question is, how can you get from a submissive or aggressive position to one of assertiveness? The first step is to think assertively.

## THINK ASSERTIVELY

Assertiveness is not selfish. It is a way of ensuring that everyone in any situation is satisfied with the outcome. It ensures that others' needs are met and their rights maintained. In order to act assertively, you have to believe that you have a right to do so. It is no good thinking highly of yourself in private but, when you come up against other people, yielding to them all the time. You have to be convinced that you — and everyone else — have certain rights which apply at both a personal and work level.

### My eight personal rights

1. To express my opinions and values and have them listened to.

2. To express my feelings and have them listened to.

3. To express my needs and have them listened to.

4. To ask for what I want.

5. To refuse a request.

6. To make choices based on my needs and wants, without having to justify them.

7. To have needs and wants that may be different from those of other people.

8. To choose not to be assertive if I do not want to be.

Let us look at these in more detail in order that you are clear about what each of these rights means.

1. *To express my opinions and values and have them listened to.*

2. *To express my feelings and have them listened to.*

3. *To express my needs and have them listened to.*

These three all involve making some kind of personal statement and insisting that it be listened to. If you are not used to saying what you think and how you feel, then you may be ignored or not taken seriously at first.

Do not be put off. Once you believe that it is acceptable to think differently from other people — that it does not make you any less of a person — then it is easier to do. If what you say hurts others, then analyse why it has this effect. It may be that they are not used to your being assertive. It may be they are used to getting their own way! It is important to care what others think and feel, but it is equally important not to care too much, because this results in denial of your own needs.

4.  *To ask for what I want.*

Asking allows the other person the same option. You are not demanding but neither are you saying nothing and hoping they will realise what you want — without having to tell them. Asking for what you want opens up the discussion in order that you can find out what the other person's needs are too, and whether they are in harmony or conflict with yours.

5.  *To refuse a request.*

This is difficult, as many women either feel guilty or think they must do something to compensate for a refusal. Many people, when making a request, do not really expect the answer 'no'; therefore saying 'no' is doubly difficult. You need to remember that when you say no, you are refusing the request but not rejecting the person. And that applies when your own requests are refused as well.

6.  *To have needs and wants that may be different from those of other people.*

7.  *To make choices based on my needs and wants, without having to justify them.*

Recognising these rights reinforces the idea of yourself as a unique individual. They free you from the constraints of the way you have always acted in the past and how other people believe you should act now.

8.  *To choose not to be assertive if I do not want to be.*

Although assertiveness is the best operating position for effective behaviour, there is a choice about whether to be assertive or not. In certain circumstances, a submissive stance may be more appropriate. Knowing when to be assertive and when not to be makes for personal effectiveness.

Choosing not to be assertive is fine — as long as it is your own choice and you have not been manipulated into that position.

If you have rights, you also have responsibilities. Each of the personal rights discussed so far is coupled with responsibilities.

## Rights and responsibilities

Right:

1. *To express my opinions and values and have them listened to.*

2. *To express my feelings and have them listened to.*

3. *To express my needs and have them listened to.*

Responsibility:

- *To express myself clearly.*
- *To be responsible for the consequences.*
- *To listen to others.*

Right:

4. *To ask for what I want.*

Responsibility:

- *To accept that I may not get what I want.*
- *To allow others to ask for what they want.*

Right:

5. *To refuse a request.*

Responsibility:

- *To make sure that the asker realises that I am refusing the request and not rejecting the person.*

Right:

6. *To make choices based on my needs and wants, without having to justify them.*

7. *To have needs and wants that may be different from those of other people.*

Responsibility:

■ *Not to damage other people either emotionally or physically (hurting someone's feelings is not real damage).*

Right:

8.  *To choose not to be assertive if I do not want to be.*

Responsibility:

■ *To be responsible for the consequences.*

As well as personal rights, you also have rights at work.

### My nine rights at work

1.  To know what is expected of me.

2.  To have regular feedback on my performance.

3.  To make mistakes sometimes without constantly having to pay for them.

4.  To be consulted about decisions that affect me.

5.  To take decisions that are within my area of work.

6.  To refuse unreasonable requests.

7.  To expect work of a certain standard from my staff.

8.  To criticise constructively the performance of my staff when appropriate.

9.  To ask for information when I need it.

**From that list, consider the rights you do not have at work but which you want.**

The rights I do not have that I would like, and that I am going to discuss with my manager:

You can discuss this with your manager later — once you have looked at how to speak assertively.

This is a good exercise to try with your team. Get them to consider the rights they do not have and discuss their responses. You may not always like what you hear, but it is a good team-building exercise.

Before you can say what you feel, you must be sure of the connection between the thinking and speaking process. Look at the following diagram.

**Right and wrong thinking**

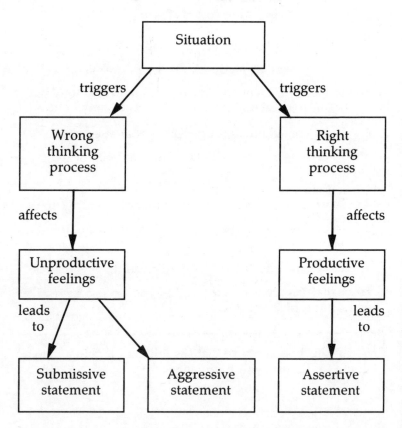

In any situation, thoughts and feelings are triggered. If these are unproductive, non-assertive thoughts, they will be followed by an aggressive or submissive statement. The only way to be able to make an assertive statement is to:

- believe you have the right to do so;
- acknowledge your rights in that particular situation.

Here are three situations and some 'wrong thinking' which leads to an aggressive or submissive statement. For each situation, decide what your rights are and write down an example of 'right thinking'. Refer to the lists of personal rights at work.

Here is an example.

**Example**

| Situation | Wrong thinking | Right thinking |
|---|---|---|
| **You are at a meeting to discuss changes in departmental practices. You are interrupted in midflow by a colleague who disagrees with you.** | How rude — I hadn't finished. Well, they can decide what they like — I won't go along with it.<br><br>or<br><br>Perhaps he's right. Senior managers know what they're talking about. | I have a right to state my opinion and be listened to. I have a point worth making. |

Remember, it is the thought process at this stage that is shown — not what you will actually say out loud.

## Situation 1

| Situation | Wrong thinking | Right thinking |
|---|---|---|
| **You have always worked late when requested, but this time you have been asked to attend a meeting which clashes with an important personal engagement.** | Well, I'll have to tell them I'm not going to this meeting and they can like it or lump it!<br><br>or<br><br>Perhaps I could go. I don't want them to think I'm unreliable. | |

## Situation 2

| Situation | Wrong thinking | Right thinking |
|---|---|---|
| **A colleague at work is always stealing your ideas. There is a promotion in the offing, and you are just as keen as she to get it. At the next meeting, she starts to put forward, as her own, ideas which you had dis-cussed together. This is the last straw.** | I'll have a quiet word with her. It didn't do the trick last time.<br><br>or<br><br>I'm going to say that it's my idea and that she's trying to claim the credit. | |

**Situation 3**

| Situation | Wrong thinking | Right thinking |
|---|---|---|
| **You are at a meeting to discuss setting up a performance appraisal system at work. You put forward what you think is a good suggestion for making employees receptive to the idea, and before you have finished speaking, someone else butts in to make a completely different point.** | Perhaps it wasn't such a good idea!<br><br>or<br><br>What am I? Just a blot on the landscape? They can decide what they like — I won't cooperate! | |

Here are some possible responses showing 'right thinking'.

*Situation 1*

Right thinking:

- *I have a right to refuse the request, which is unreasonable.*
- *I have a right to have needs and wants that are different from those of other people.*
- *I have a right to be consulted about the timing of meetings if it is important that I attend.*
- *I have a right to ask for information about the meeting and how important my presence is.*
- *I have the right to make choices based on my wants and needs.*

*Situation 2*

Right thinking:

- *I have the right to express how I feel about this.*
- *I have the right to ask for what I want to happen.*

*Situation 3*

Right thinking:

- *I have a right to express my opinion.*
- *I have the right to be listened to.*
- *I have a right to be consulted about decisions that affect me.*

Notice how many times the rights to express wants, needs and feelings are identified. It is important that you start to think about your rights in every situation before you decide what to say.

## SPEAK ASSERTIVELY

As a manager, you will have to speak assertively in many situations. Here are some of the main circumstances which may arise and some strategies to help.

### Circumstance 1 — making requests

When making requests, at any level, you need to keep uppermost in mind that you have a right to ask, and the other person has a right to refuse or, if not refuse, point out the difficulties that the request may cause.

The way you ask is important. The two basic rules are these:

- Keep it short.
- Explain why.

Keeping it short requires that you express yourself very clearly; explaining your reasons shows why you are making the request and how important it is. For example, 'I need this month's figures for the departmental meeting next week. Could I have them by Friday?'

Here are five things you must never do when making requests.

## Making requests

1. **Don't** apologise. For example: 'I'm really sorry to bother you.'

2. **Don't** hint. For example: 'You aren't going down the high street, by any chance. I'd love a drink.'

3. **Don't** be long-winded. For example: 'I know you're very busy today and this report must be the last thing on your mind but . . .'

4. **Don't** flatter. For example: 'You're so good at doing these reports . . .'

5. **Don't** manipulate. For example: 'Be an angel and . . ., I'd be so grateful if you . . .'

### Circumstance 2 — stating what you want to happen

Stating what you want to happen means you are exercising your rights to be taken seriously, listened to, or consulted.

## The three-line strategy

**Line 1**   Let people know that you are listening and appreciate their position.

- 'I hear what you are saying . . .'
- 'I understand why you feel . . .'
- 'I realise that . . .'
- 'I know you don't mean anything by it, but . . .'

**Line 2**   State how you feel or what you think. Be simple, direct and polite. Use 'I'.

- 'I feel . . .'
- 'I think . . .'

**Line 3**   State what you want or what action you want to be taken.

- 'I would like . . .'
- 'I want . . .'
- 'I don't want . . .'
- 'What about . . .'
- 'How would you feel about . . . ?'
- 'Would it help to . . . ?'

## Circumstance 3 — refusing requests

There are four steps you can take when refusing requests.

*Step 1: Be direct*

Some women feel that saying 'no' is too direct. There are other ways.

- 'I don't want to . . .'
- 'I prefer not to . . .'
- 'I'd rather not . . .'
- 'I'm not happy to . . .'
- 'It's not possible . . .'

Do not say 'I can't because . . .'. That leads to your being unable to refuse if the 'because' part of your refusal can be sorted out! Moreover, it sounds like an excuse and that you accept that you really ought to agree to the request.

*Step 2: Give a reason*

Giving a simple reason explains your position to the asker and sounds less abrupt than a straight 'no'. Here are two examples:

REQUEST: 'Shall we go for a walk?'
**RESPONSE:** 'I don't want to — it's too cold.'

REQUEST: 'Can you stay late tomorrow?'
**RESPONSE:** 'I'd rather not — I'm meeting someone after work.'

*Step 3: Apologise only if you are sorry*

Many women apologise profusely — often! They begin a refusal with 'I'm awfully sorry, but . . .'. Apologise only if you are genuinely sorry that you cannot do what someone has asked, and but for x, y, or z, you would have been glad to do it. Then an apology is sincere. Here is an example:

REQUEST: 'Can you give me a lift into town?'
**RESPONSE:** 'I'm sorry, I can't, as I'm not going into town tonight. I have to pick John up.'

If you are genuinely sorry that you cannot help, apologising is a way of expressing this. If you are not sorry, an assertive response to that request would be:

**RESPONSE:** 'It's not possible tonight — I have to pick John up.'

If you want to express regret without saying the word 'sorry':

**RESPONSE:** 'It's not possible tonight — I have to pick John up. Otherwise I would be glad to.'

It is a good idea to adopt this way of expressing regret in preference to saying the word 'sorry' — cut out that word altogether.

*Step 4: Examine possibilities*

Here you need to explore the issues a bit more. You might want more information about the request — how urgent it is; does it have to be done by you? You might want to explain the consequences for you, or suggest possibilities. What this does is to show askers that you are concerned about their situation, while not giving in to their requests. For example:

- 'I could do it tomorrow instead.'
- 'Which of my other tasks shall I leave to get this done?'
- 'If I do this, I won't get the figures complete for the meeting on Monday.'

Now, to put the theory into practice.

**Go back to the situations on right thinking. Now you need to translate your right thinking into assertive statements. In each case, write down the statement you would make.**

Remember:

- I understand . . .
- I feel . . .
- I would like . . .

*Situation 1*

You have always worked late when requested, but this time you have been asked to attend a meeting which clashes with an important personal engagement.

```
Assertive statement:



```

*Situation 2*

A colleague at work is always stealing your ideas. There is a promotion in the offing and you are just as keen as she to get it. At the next meeting, she starts to put forward, as her own, ideas which you had discussed together. This is the last straw.

```
Assertive statement:


```

*Situation 3*

You are at a meeting to discuss setting up a performance appraisal system at work. You put forward what you think is a good suggestion for making employees receptive to the idea. Before you have finished speaking, someone else butts in to make a completely different point.

Assertive statement:

Here are some suggested responses.

*Situation 1*

> I realise we've a lot of work on, but it's not possible for me to work tonight. I've an important personal engagement. Would it help if I stayed tomorrow night?

If you begin by saying, 'I realise we've a lot of work on', you cannot be accused of misunderstanding the situation. Also, you do usually work late when requested. Remember that you have the right to refuse an unreasonable request; you do not have to justify it and give detailed explanations about why you cannot stay, nor do you have to say you are sorry, but, quite simply, say 'It's not possible'. However, in certain circumstances such as this case, it can be helpful if you can offer some sort of compromise.

*Situation 2*

> I'm glad Jane has raised the ideas that we came up with together. There are one or two points I would like to add.

This is the response you would make if you were actually at the meeting. Even if you felt that it was inappropriate to tackle Jane about it in front of everybody else, you would want to make the point at the meeting that these ideas came from both of you. But if you want to make a point to Jane alone, then you could say:

> I realise you may not know you are doing it, but putting forward our ideas as if they were your own is making me angry. In future, I'd like both our names to go on the bottom of the report, and the presentation to be done jointly.

By beginning, 'I realise you may not be aware you are doing it', you are avoiding making an accusation which can be denied by somebody's saying, 'I didn't mean to do that', or 'I didn't realise I was doing it'. By giving others the benefit of the doubt, you may go on to say how you feel about it and what you want to happen. You are not blaming the person; you are just stating the situation.

*Situation 3*

> 'I know you want to make a point, Keith, but I think the issue of performance appraisal is a crucial one, and I would like to finish the point I was making.'

If you accompany this statement by looking at Keith, using his name, and perhaps using some non-verbal signals (such as making a slight pushing movement with your hands at waist level), Keith will register and respond to your signals.

Once you have finished making your point, turn back and say, 'Now, Keith, what was the point you wanted to make?' The objective here is to finish your point and stop him from interrupting you; therefore you have to be quick and assertive. Do not pause in the middle, and give Keith a chance to say, 'Oh! Well, I'm sorry', or 'Well, go on then' or 'Well, I just thought'.

Finally, we come to one of the most difficult aspects of speaking assertively — giving criticism.

### Circumstance 4 — giving criticism

If you have ever been criticised, and it would be unusual if you have not, you will readily understand how it feels to be criticised badly. It is important to bear this in mind when you have to criticise members of your staff. If criticism is to be given in a constructive manner, with the intention of improving the performance of a member of staff, it should be given in a direct, fair and assertive way. This means that you accept that, as a manager, you have the right — and the responsibility — to give criticism when it is warranted.

## Giving criticism — step by step

*Step 1: Choose the time and place*

Always make sure that criticism is given in private and as soon after the event as possible. People learn to overcome their mistakes more quickly when the actual details of what they did are fresh in their minds.

*Step 2: Introduce the topic directly*

Do not beat about the bush. Say briefly what it is you want to talk about and how the matter has arisen. Always introduce the topic with a first-person statement: 'I want to . . .', 'I need to . . .', 'I would like to . . .'. Such a statement puts you in control.

*Step 3: State the problem*

Remember the importance of criticising the behaviour — not the person. Pinpoint those aspects of the person's performance which are causing problems. Be precise and, no matter how angry you feel, do not generalise, as in:

- 'There were a lot of errors in the accounts.'
- 'Forgetting to send out the reports causes a lot of problems.'
- 'You have been late on several occasions this week.'

If you feel that you need to emphasise the gravity of the situation, it may help to make criticised people aware of the consequences of their problem behaviour upon you, upon your staff, or upon themselves.

*Step 4: Ask for a response*

Give people an opportunity to explain or to state their perception of the situation — and make sure that you listen attentively to what they say. Use open questions such as:

- 'How do you see this?'
- 'Is that a valid assessment of the situation?'
- 'Do you wish to say anything?'

The criticised person may offer a valid excuse or explanation. You will then need to modify or withdraw your criticism. To carry on criticising in the face of alternative information is aggressive. If the person agrees with you, you have the basis for a discussion on how the problem has arisen and what both of you can do about it. If the person says nothing, you may have to probe a little deeper. Try not to get irritated in the face of obstinacy, and move on to try to reach a negotiated solution.

*Step 5: Negotiate a solution*

Ask the person being criticised for suggestions as to how improvements could be made. If he or she has difficulties in doing this, you could offer some suggestions:

- 'How about . . . ?'
- 'Do you think you could . . . ?'

There will be a greater commitment to follow through solutions, if the people responsible for the behaviour have identified it for themselves.

*Step 6: State the agreed solution*

Summarise all that has been said and agreed upon. If a task is to be performed, make sure that you specify the standards that you require and, if appropriate, a deadline for completion. Get the other person's agreement to what has been decided. It is at this final stage, before the person leaves, that you should ensure that there are no obstacles to good performance.

When giving criticism in this assertive manner, remember to keep your non-verbal communication assertive, too: no smiles to appease the person you are criticising; no hand-wringing to betray your nervousness; no aggressive finger-pointing.

**Communicating with confidence means communicating assertively.**

## 2

# Good Communication

Communication is the management skill which underpins all others. Organisations need managers with good communication skills — to motivate people; to instruct, counsel and advise; to build effective teams; to negotiate fairly; to develop the potential of their staff; and to relate to people at all levels both inside and outside the organisation.

When it comes to good communication, women have particular strengths; strengths which are sometimes not recognised by women themselves or the organisation they work for.

This chapter analyses the communication process and assesses the ways in which people communicate. It also looks at ways of improving verbal and non-verbal communication.

## THE COMMUNICATION PROCESS

To begin with, what can you do to make certain that your messages are understood and acted upon? There are six steps in the process of effective communication.

### Six steps in the communication process

1. Know your purpose, strategy and message.

2. Identify your target audience.

3. Overcome the barriers.

4. Select the appropriate type and style of communication.

5. Transmit the message.

6. Obtain feedback.

Only when you have successfully completed each of the six steps, can you be sure that your communication was effective. Now let us examine the six steps in more detail.

## Know your purpose, strategy and message

Even before you begin to communicate, you should ask yourself, 'What exactly am I trying to achieve? What do I want the receiver to know, do, or consider as a result of my communication?' This is the purpose of your communication.

Having decided on the outcome you want, you can plan your strategy. Do you need to give information, to instruct, to motivate, to discuss, or to assess? The answers to these questions will depend on your purpose, and on your assessment of the situation.

For example, let us suppose that your secretary is always late in typing the minutes of committee meetings. What you want to achieve is a copy of the minutes on the desk of every member of the committee within a week of the meeting. How will you go about it? If you have not made your requirements clear in the past, you may need simply to inform. If you think it is a scheduling problem, you may need to give some instruction. If it is a case of being uncooperative, you may need to motivate and/or discipline. Assessing the situation and defining your purpose and your strategy help you to word your message more appropriately.

## Identify your target audience

You know what you want to achieve. But have you considered how your message might be received? Reception of messages is affected by education, past experience, skills, knowledge, age, gender, race and values.

First of all, you will need to consider whether your target audience is capable of understanding your message. Remember:

- Some people find it hard to take in a lot of information at one time.
- Practical people may find it hard to grasp new ideas.
- People used to routine may find it hard to cope with new procedures.
- Lack of confidence makes it hard to listen in what appears to be a new and threatening situation.

At another level — and this will apply only to someone with whom you are in regular contact and know well — other personal factors affect the recipient's motivation to do what you want. If you can tailor your message to fit in with a person's interests, you are more likely to achieve your ends. Either way, knowing your target audience will help you to communicate appropriately and effectively.

But, first, whom do you communicate with at work? You are now going to try to summarise the communication process you use with your most regular contacts.

**On the Communication chart which follows, fill in the left-hand column with the names and positions of people you have regular contact with at work. Ignore the last three columns for now. We shall come back to those later.**

Opposite is an example, broken down into departments.

You will come back to the chart a little later. For now, move on to the next step in the communication process.

## Overcome the barriers

There are a number of barriers to effective communication. At the simplest level, physical conditions can be a barrier. If you try to talk in a place which is too cold, noisy, or uncomfortable, or in which you are constantly interrupted, you will not get very far. There are a number of other barriers which have nothing to do with the physical environment, but which can be overcome relatively easily.

*Barrier 1 — gender*

As a woman, you could find this to be your biggest barrier. Certain people are unused to women in positions of authority

## Communication chart

| Contact | Barriers | Type | Style |
|---|---|---|---|
| In my department:<br>　Secretary — Mary<br>　Team leader — Geoff<br>　Field officer — Dianne<br><br>Other departments:<br>1. Publications<br>　　Head — Joe<br>　　Printer — Michael<br>2. Library<br>　　Head — Ewan<br>　　Assistant — Nadir | | | |

## Communication chart

| Contact | Barriers | Type | Style |
|---|---|---|---|
| | | | |

and are unsure of how to respond to them. It is even more difficult if the woman is young and well qualified. Men, particularly those who are used to seeing women in supportive roles, may find it threatening to have a woman in charge.

Moreover, women may be seen by men as mother or daughter figures, or potential sexual partners, rather than as colleagues or managers. Therefore, women may find it difficult to get such men to take them seriously.

One way of overcoming this barrier is to get the issue into the open. Get your staff together and ask how many have worked for a woman. Ask those who have not done so, what their expectations are. Your willingness to listen will go a long way towards dispelling anger and suspicion.

### Barrier 2 — age

Older people who have been with an organisation a long time may find it difficult to respond to a younger person as their superior. You could help to smooth ruffled feathers by using their good practice as a model where possible. Ask for their opinions and ideas regularly, and give them areas of special responsibility. On the other hand, young people who have just left home may find it difficult to relate to you as an older person, because they see you as the mother from whom they are trying to be independent.

You may find it easier to talk to people of your own age than to either of these groups. However, your peers may want to talk to you as an equal and expect you to do likewise; that is, not to exert your authority.

Whatever people's age, you should treat them honestly and respectfully, and take them seriously,

You also need to remember that if you want to achieve your objectives, it is more important to be respected than to be liked. If you are liked as well, so much the better. But people will not work well for someone they do not respect.

### Barrier 3 — status

Sometimes the mere fact of your having a high status can create a barrier between you and the more insecure juniors. The barrier can be heightened if you use a style of leadership different from the one they are used to; for example, if you are a 'democratic' leader, working with a team who are used to an 'authoritarian' head, or vice versa. Again, you need to bring the issue out into the open, if you feel there is a barrier. Talking to staff about their attitudes to authority and status can ease the situation.

*Barrier 4 — personal attitudes*

These are your own feelings towards the status and authority you hold and your attitudes generally. Do you hold strong opinions about most things? Are there any kinds of people about whom you have prejudices? Everyone has different ideas about what is right and what is wrong, and this in itself is not the problem. The problem is the potential communication barrier with people you feel uncomfortable with or disapprove of.

You need to identify all these groups, and in your dealings with them, you must be careful not to let your feelings show.

*Barrier 5 — socio-cultural/language differences*

People of different cultures and social classes may assign different meaning to gestures, work or forms of behaviour. Some are more formal than others, and some use different expressions to describe the same thing. In many organisations, professional jargon can be a major obstacle. If you are at cross purposes with others, ask yourself: 'Am I using the wrong words to describe this? Can they understand what I'm saying?' Or, conversely, 'Are they using these words in the same way that I would? Am I getting and giving the right message?'

**Now turn back to the Communication chart and complete the second column. That is, for each of the people with whom you communicate regularly, make a note of any barriers, including physical ones.**

There is an example of communication barriers overleaf.

If you find you are having communication problems with any of your staff, whether junior or senior, male or female, of whatever social class or culture, you need to:

- take time to talk about the barrier with the person concerned;
- talk it through with other colleagues;
- make a commitment to work on it.

Now that you have identified the purpose, target audiences, and barriers, you must choose the best communication medium to get your message across.

## Communication chart

| Contact | Barriers | Type | Style |
|---|---|---|---|
| In my department:<br>  Secretary | young, shy, conscious of my status and afraid of it. | | |
|   Team leader | male, pompous, intense. | | |
|   Field officer | none — woman of similar age, background and interests. | | |
| Other departments:<br>1. Publications | department noisy, hard to concentrate there. | | |
|   Head | male chauvinist — but kindly rather than pompous.<br>Too easy to fall into 'little girl' role. | | |
|   Printer | male, young, attractive (and knows it!) sexual innuendos. | | |
| 2. Library | problem of having to be quiet. | | |
|   Head | none — easy going man of similar background. | | |
|   Assistant | older woman — resents me and her head for being young, well qualified, better paid and because we get on well — she is frighteningly efficient and lets us know it! | | |

## Select the appropriate type and style of communication

The method you use to communicate your message is important, as is the style you adopt.

*Types of communication*

The three most common methods of communication are verbal, written and telephone. Before you can select the appropriate type of communication, it is important to be aware of the advantages and disadvantages of each.

*Verbal communication*

| Advantages | Disadvantages |
| --- | --- |
| This is more natural, more involving, and less bureau-cratic than the written word. | The very directness of the message and immediacy of the feedback can be threat-ening. |
| It allows the speaker to take account of feedback and refine the message accord-ingly. | The immediate feedback may interrupt your line of thought. |
| It is immediate — ideas, plans, suggestions can be acted on immediately. | You may be let down by your own unconscious non-verbal behaviour. |
| It can be supplemented with non-verbal communi-cation. | If you need to contact many people, it can be inefficient. |

*Telephone communication*

| Advantages | Disadvantages |
| --- | --- |
| It gives you speed of access to people and information. | It is less personal. |
| You are not so likely to be let down by your unconscious non-verbal behaviour — only your tone or pitch of voice can be significant. | The distortion of the human voice can lead to misunderstandings. |
| | You will not be able to supplement what you say with non-verbal behaviour. |

*Written communication*

| Advantages | Disadvantages |
|---|---|
| Details of what you want to 'say' can be thought through before you say it. | Delayed feedback means you have to word your message appropriately. |
| It communicates without interruption. | Some people have difficulties with grammar, spelling, style or organisation. |
| You can reach large numbers of people simultaneously. | It is the most formal means of communication. |
| Records can be kept. | You have no control over who sees/hears your message. |

### Styles of communication

Whichever medium you select as the most appropriate for the communication, your style is also important. Style means the degree of formality used. The style you use depends on a number of factors, including personality, target audience, purpose and strategy, and speed of action.

### Personality

Some people, particularly women, prefer to use the informal approach wherever possible. Others feel that the formal approach is needed to distance themselves from their subordinates and maintain their authority.

Even if your predominant style is formal, remember that building up informal networks can be invaluable for speeding up lines of communication. For example, if your daughter is in the same class as the daughter of the secretary in administration, then meeting informally at school functions could prove an advantage if you need supplies quickly!

*Target audience*

If the person with whom you are communicating feels threatened by you, or by what you are going to say, an informal verbal approach is much the best way to communicate.

*Purpose and strategy*

When giving criticism, a formal style is called for. If you wish to persuade or motivate someone, an informal approach is usually more suitable.

*Speed of action required*

Generally speaking, the quicker the action is required, the more formal the style. In urgent situations, there will be no time for informal pleasantries, and your style will reflect this.

Now for some practice in appropriate communication.

**Go back to the Communication chart and note the best type and style of communication for each contact. Choose from verbal, telephone or written, and from formal or informal. If you use the whole range with some contacts, then write them down.**

There is an example of a completed chart overleaf.

Each person's pattern is unique. No one can say that you should always communicate in a particular way. But you do need to be aware of your pattern and to be sure you are choosing from strength rather than weakness; that is, you are choosing a type or style that suits you and the situation, rather than avoiding ones you find difficult.

The next stage in the communication process is getting your message across.

**Transmit the message**

In transmitting your message, you should follow these rules:

- take time to do it properly;
- be clear and exact in what you say;
- be consistent and logical;

## Communication chart

| Contact | Barriers | Type | Style |
|---|---|---|---|
| **In my department:** Secretary | young, shy, conscious of my status and afraid of it. | verbal | informal |
| Team leader | male, pompous, intense. | verbal | informal |
| Field officer | none — woman of similar age, background and interests. | verbal | informal |
| **Other departments:** 1. Publications | department noisy, hard to concentrate there. | | |
| Head | male chauvinist — but kindly rather than pompous. Too easy to fall into 'little girl' rôle. | verbal telephone | informal |
| Printer | male, young, attractive (and knows it!) sexual innuendos. | verbal telephone | informal |
| 2. Library | — problem of having to be quiet. | | |
| Head | none — easy going man of similar background. | verbal | informal — sometimes formal when collaborating a project. |
| Assistant | older woman — resents me and her head for being young, well-qualified, better paid and because we get on well — she is frighteningly efficient and let us know it! | telephone written | formal |

- keep it relevant, say all you need but no more;
- give reasons, if necessary;
- be discreet.

And the final stage of getting feedback ensures that you have got your message across.

## Obtain feedback

Asking for feedback is essential to effective communication, for, when you know how the message is received, you can refine it, if necessary. You will need to establish not only that your message has been received, but also that it has been understood and, even more importantly, accepted; that is, the recipient acts in the way you wish.

To summarise, effective communication is a six-stage process:

1.  Know your purpose, strategy and message.

2.  Identify your target audience.

3.  Overcome the barriers.

4.  Select the appropriate type and style of communication.

5.  Transmit the message.

6.  Obtain feedback.

So far you have looked at the overall process of communication in terms of getting your message across. Now let us look at verbal communication in more detail.

## PLAIN SPEAKING

As stated earlier, verbal communication has distinct advantages over other forms:

- It is more natural, and less bureaucratic.
- It makes people feel they have been consulted personally.
- It allows senders to take account of the responses they get and therefore helps them to get the message across more effectively.
- It can be supported by non-verbal communication.
- It enables the sharing and comparing of ideas and feelings.

To benefit from these advantages, you need to be skilled in the art. Verbal communications can be a minefield of confusion and misunderstanding. Consider the following examples of illogic and self-contradiction.

*He has waited 62 years to meet the brother he never knew he had.*
**BBC News Reporter**

*Has there ever been any link between asbestos and asbestos-linked diseases?*
**Jimmy Young**

*We welcome back long-wave listeners and apologise for the 20-minute break in transmission. We hope it didn't spoil your enjoyment of 'Thirty-Minute Theatre'.*
**Announcer, BBC Radio 4**

*What do you do?*
*Contestant: I'm a housewife and mother.*
*Simon Bates: Got any kids?*
**Simon Bates**

*I turned to see all the onlookers looking on.*
**Anneka Rice**

*. . . and, somewhat surprisingly, Cambridge have won the toss.*
**Harry Carpenter**

*Don't tell those coming in now the result of that fantastic match. Now let's have another look at Italy's winning goal.*
**David Coleman**

*How priceless are these things?*
**Russell Harty**

*Well, clearly, Graeme, it all went according to plan — what was the plan exactly?*
**Elton Wellsby**

Sometimes, confusing words or sentences can have unfortunate results, and your staff could end up feeling very resentful if you have given them instructions or information which turns out to be incomplete or misleading.

You probably use verbal communications more than any other form. Check your Communication chart and you will probably find that most exchanges you have with your regular contacts are verbal ones.

Verbal communications, then, are likely to be important to you in your job and one aspect is paramount — that of giving instructions.

## Giving instructions

For some women, this is a difficult area. Firstly, some women may feel uneasy in a role which involves telling others what to do, perhaps because in the past they have been in the position of being told what to do by others. Secondly, they fear that what they have to say may not be well received. This means they may not be popular, may not be liked — and many women find this difficult to cope with. Moreover, many men — and women too — do not easily accept a woman in a leadership role. Her authority may be questioned and her instructions ignored. The task of giving effective instructions is, therefore, of great importance.

To help you overcome any difficulty, here is an eight-step procedure you can use when giving instructions.

### Eight steps for giving instructions

1. Take time.
2. Be clear.
3. Be consistent and logical.
4. Be relevant.
5. Explain why.
6. Be discreet.
7. Ask for feedback.
8. Remember your non-verbal communication.

*Step 1   Make time*

Before you give instructions, make certain you have enough time to do it properly. This should include time for feedback and further explanation if necessary. Try to ensure that you will not be interrupted. Instructions shouted over your shoulder as you dash through the door are not likely to be taken in — or taken seriously.

*Step 2   Be clear*

This means keeping it simple and saying exactly what you mean. Try to avoid abbreviations and jargon. The world of computers is a good example of an industry where such language is used all the time. Expressions such as 'IT', 'floppy', 'VDU' and 'hardware' can all lead to confusion for someone who does not fully understand the system. If everyone concerned knows the jargon, that is all right. Problems arise when someone involved in the discussion does not fully understand, and that happens often, because it takes a confident person to ask, 'Would you explain what you are talking about, please?'

Abbreviations can be a very convenient, shorthand way of communicating with other people who know them. But they will be incomprehensible to those who do not. In addition, using abbreviations can make the recipients feel inferior, because they cannot work out what is going on. Thus, the overuse of abbreviations says, 'I know all about this matter, and you don't. I've got the power in this situation, and don't you forget it.'

Jargon, on the other hand, is simply a device for making the relatively simple sound agonisingly complex. It is another area where all sorts of confusion and mixed signals can arise. Some professionals feel the need to guard their territory against outsiders — and a very effective way of keeping others out is to mystify them.

As well as avoiding abbreviations and jargon, you must be as clear as possible; otherwise, instructions will be misinterpreted.

Try the following exercise with a friend or colleague, to determine how precise you are at giving instructions.

Give your partner a pencil and paper. Keep the drawing shown opposite hidden from view. Describe it using words alone — no hand signals! Ask your partner to construct the drawing from your verbal description.

Describe each step in one clear statement; for example: 'From the left end of the line draw a perpendicular line 2

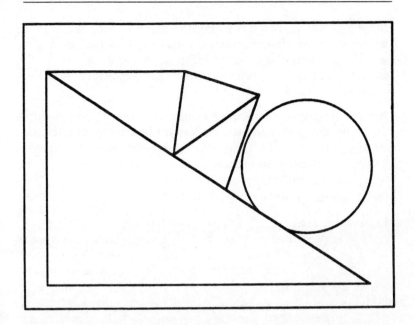

inches in length.' Do not revise or correct your description once you have made it, and do not look at what your partner draws in response to each instruction. Your partner is not allowed to ask questions. When your partner's drawing is finished, compare it with the drawing above. How precise was your verbal description?

Now let us look at the third step for giving instructions, bearing in mind how much room there is for improvement!

### Step 3  *Be consistent and logical*

Being consistent and logical means planning in advance what you are going to say. If there are a number of key points to make in your instruction, you should number them and put them in a logical order. This will be useful when summarising the main points at the end.

### Step 4  *Be relevant*

This means giving all the necessary information and only the necessary information. It includes details of:

- when something has to be done;
- to what standards something has to be done;
- any particular way something has to be done;
- all the tools, whether information or resources, in order that the job is done effectively.

Although you must include all the necessary information, you must be careful not to give any more information than is strictly necessary. The less there is to remember, the more likely it is to be remembered.

### Step 5   Explain why

Explaining why you want someone to do something not only clarifies the message, but also reinforces it. 'Explain why' includes the consequences of not carrying out your instructions properly. Listeners should not have to work out which are the important bits of the message. For example, if you ask someone to send out the minutes quickly with a note attached, he or she may not know whether it is more important to send the minutes out with a handwritten note attached in order to catch that night's post, or whether they must have a typewritten note and not go out until the following day.

### Step 6   Be discreet

Discretion is an important personal quality which will become more and more important as you move up the managerial scale. Part of being discreet is to use the appropriate language for the appropriate person and occasion; you looked at this topic earlier.

A good rule of thumb is never to name names or gossip about company concerns with subordinates or outsiders. Be guarded; be discreet. Your staff will respect you for it.

### Step 7   Ask for feedback

As with all communication, when you give instructions or information, get feedback to ascertain if the other person has understood what you have been saying. And this is why the first step is important — if you are getting feedback, allow yourself enough time to listen. If you are in a rush to do something else, it is the feedback that will be sacrificed. Yet the feedback is the only indication you have that your message has been fully understood.

You also need to give your recipients time to ask questions of you. Do not rush on with 'fine' and 'right' and 'good', assuming that all is well. All might not be fine, and right, and good, but by rushing on you do not give anyone a chance to say so. Getting the answer 'Yes' to the question 'Do you understand?' is not obtaining adequate feedback. Ask the listener to repeat the instructions back to you. You could say, 'Do you want to go through it for me while I'm here so I can make sure I've included everything you need to know?'

*Step 8   Remember your non-verbal communication*

Make sure your non-verbal communication does not contradict your verbal message. If you are saying how important it is that this report reach your boss's desk by midday, then you should not look down and fiddle with something on your desk before smiling. Do not forget the strength of those non-verbal messages.

## NON-VERBAL COMMUNICATION

It has been estimated that more than two-thirds of communication is non-verbal, and that in cases where the verbal and non-verbal messages conflict, it is the non-verbal message which dominates.

Women are often said to be good at interpreting other people's body language, but not very good at managing their own. For example, they are more likely to make nervous gestures, to smile inappropriately, to remain silent rather than provoke confrontation, and to use a tone of voice which men find difficult to listen to. All these can count against women who wish to be seen as effective leaders at work, since they reinforce the stereotype of the passive female.

Such habits can also hinder communication because of the mixed messages they send. Persisting in inappropriate non-verbal behaviour means having to accept that your words will probably be ignored.

The following exercise asks you to assess the signals given out by non-verbal communication.

**Opposite are ten descriptions of behaviour. Write in the box the messages you think could be conveyed by a person who behaves as described. Use 'I' statements from the sender's perspective, eg 'I am confident', 'I don't like you', or 'I am lying'.**

1. Does not look at you when speaking to you.

**Message:**

2. Moves closer to you when listening to you.

**Message:**

3. Touches you lightly but deliberately on the arm.

**Message:**

4. Takes off glasses and flings them on the table.

**Message:**

5. Walks into a meeting and sits at the back.

**Message:**

6.   Tilts head and smiles.

**Message:**

7.   Covers mouth with hand while speaking.

**Message:**

8.   Walks purposefully into a room, looking straight ahead.

**Message:**

9.   Smiles when making a complaint.

**Message:**

10.   Wears a navy, pinstripe suit.

**Message:**

Here are some possible interpretations of these acts.

### Interpreting non-verbal communication

1.  Not making eye contact can be interpreted to mean a number of things, including:

    — I do not like you.
    — I am not sure of what I am saying.
    — I feel guilty.
    — I am hiding something.
    — I do not feel confident.
    — I am not interested.
    — I do not want to hurt you.
    — I am embarrassed by what you are saying.

Eyes are probably the most expressive part of body language. Be sure to use them positively.

2.  Moving closer to you can signify:

    — I am more powerful than you.
    — I am trying to intimidate you.
    — I like you.
    — I admire you.
    — I have something to tell you.
    — I cannot hear you very well.

All people have their own 'personal space' — a distance from others at which they feel comfortable. Invading the personal space of someone you do not know well can be intimidating. You need to be aware of both its positive and negative connotations.

3.  Someone who touches you lightly but deliberately on the arm could be saying:

    — I like you.
    — I am reassuring you.
    — I understand how you feel.
    — I want to reinforce what I am saying.
    — I am more powerful than you.
    — I am your superior.

Touch is so sensitive a medium that it is best used only with people you know well.

4.  Flinging down glasses may mean:

    — I am angry.
    — I am exasperated.
    — I have lost control.
    — I am making a point by being aggressive.

This gesture usually signifies a momentary loss of control. An alternative response is to cry. It provides the same sort of emotional release. Is crying as socially acceptable as anger? Would the interpretation depend on whether the person was male or female? The type of aggression represented by flinging something down on a table is often seen, rightly or wrongly, as a sign of authority.

5.  Someone who walks into a meeting and sits at the back may be saying:

    — I do not have to sit at the front to be noticed.
    — I do not want to be noticed.
    — I have to leave early.
    — I am not interested in the proceedings.
    — I should not be here.

Usually, someone who does this does not want to contribute or participate. If you usually sit at the back, ask yourself why you do this. Are you happy with the impression this may give to others?

6.  Tilting the head while smiling is said to be typical of women. It transmits the following messages:

    — I am shy.
    — I am cute.
    — I lack confidence.
    — I want you to like me.

Women often do this without realising it. The danger is that if women act as if they were inferior, they will be treated as such.

7.  When you cover your mouth you are saying:

    — I am not sure of what I am saying.
    — I am nervous.

— I should not say this.
— I feel uncomfortable talking to you.

Putting your hand over your mouth weakens the impact of what you say and draws attention to your uneasiness.

8.  Walking purposefully into a room while looking straight ahead can convey:

— I know where I am going.
— I am in control of myself.
— I am a little too self-assured.
— I am above the rest of you.
— I am a little nervous, and so I am making sure that I do not catch anyone's eye.

You need to be aware that by entering a room in this way you can appear arrogant, even if you are quaking in your boots. To feel comfortable and look confident, relax your shoulders, walk at a steady pace, and glance round the room as you walk in.

9.  A smile when complaining can convey the message:

— I am laughing at you.
— I want you to like me.
— I am still a nice person, even though I am complaining.
— I like you.
— I feel uneasy.
— I feel embarrassed.

Women often smile when they complain or criticise, because they fear a hostile reaction. They want to be liked; therefore they soften the criticism. If you send conflicting messages, you confuse the recipient and will not be taken seriously.

10.  Wearing a navy, pinstripe suit may carry the message:

— I am super-efficient.
— I am a management clone.
— I am wearing this to remind you of my status.
— I want to look as if I am doing a good job.

The message again depends on the gender and status of the wearer, and on the organisational culture.

What this exercise shows is that non-verbal communication is open to a variety of interpretations. Body language is not an exact science — one gesture can mean different things to *different* people. You need to be aware of your non-verbal communication channels — otherwise, you may not convey the message you intended, even if you are *saying* all the right words.

Here are three things you can do now to improve your non-verbal communication:

1.  Watch other people — at work, at social occasions, or on television interviews. Compare the body language with the words you hear, and see how consistent or contradictory the messages are.

2.  Think about your own postures and gestures when in different moods and frames of mind; where are my hands, am I leaning forward or back, are my legs crossed, is my chin up?

3.  Learn to control your own body language so that you send only those signals you want to transmit — those which promote the things which you are saying, and those which project the image you want to project. This means you decide, firstly, what image you do want to project, and, secondly, what specific messages you want to send.

Here are some more ideas on effective communication from another woman manager.

## Case Study

Diana Balsdon, Senior Manager, National Westminster Bank, London

I think the first thing is to be interested in what is happening to staff, and encourage them to talk on an informal basis, as well as during the staff progression and development assessments.

It's important to involve staff as much as possible, so we all sit down and discuss things regularly, and I give them as much information as I can. If I can't get them to support and work with me, I can't function properly. In a changing environment people are bound to feel uneasy, so it's essential to be as open as possible so we can all go forward together.

In my job I have to talk to a whole range of people, so I think it's important to think about what my objectives are, and what I want to get out of meeting them. I try to find out as much as I can about the individual, particularly if I want to influence them. If messages aren't getting through, you have to be adaptable. For example, if a telephone message is relayed through a third person, and you're not completely comfortable that the message has got through, then it's a good idea to ring the person direct. You could say, 'I've been away for a couple of days, and I'd like to discuss the issues that I talked through with your colleague the other day.' This way you overcome any misunderstandings.

Finally, on the check-list which follows is a series of questions. Answer them for yourself, and then ask a good friend to answer them for you. You need to know what you are doing now, in order to build on strengths and improve weaknesses, so insist on the truth!

## How I communicate non-verbally

| Non-Verbal Check-list | Yes/No | I'm happy with this: write **good** I'm not happy with this: write **change** |
|---|---|---|
| Do I dress comfortably? | | |
| Do I dress appropriately for the occasion? | | |
| Do I stand up straight? | | |
| Do I always sit back in my chair? | | |
| Do I stand with my arms folded? | | |
| Do I stand with my hands on my hips? | | |
| Do I stand at an appropriate distance from the person I am speaking to? | | |
| Do I tilt my head when I talk or listen? | | |
| Do I keep my head down when I talk or listen? | | |
| Is the expression on my face often aggressive? (set jaw, clenched teeth, scowl, jutting chin) | | |
| Do I look nervous? (worried frown, apologetic smile, biting of lip) | | |

| Non-Verbal Check-list | Yes/No | I'm happy with this: write **good** I'm not happy with this: write **change** |
|---|---|---|
| Do I smile inappropriately? (when angry, complaining, criticising) | | |
| Do I wag my finger when I talk? | | |
| Do I wave my hands about when I talk? | | |
| Do I fiddle with things? (hair, necklace, earring) | | |
| Do I touch people when I talk to them? | | |
| Do I tap my feet? | | |
| Do I look at people when I talk to them? | | |
| Do I stare at people when I talk to them? | | |
| Do I speak loudly? | | |
| Do I speak softly? | | |
| Is my voice singsong? | | |
| Is my voice whining? | | |
| Do I hesitate (um) a lot? | | |

| Do I clear my throat a lot? | | |
|---|---|---|
| Do I cry at work? | | |
| Do I cover my mouth when speaking? | | |
| Do I walk into a room confidently? | | |

# Managing a Team

The benefits of effective team-building cannot be over-emphasised. Success in this area has ramifications which extend throughout the organisation. When you improve the way the team works, you improve its ability to solve problems. This, in turn, means increased efficiency which boosts morale and productivity. It also reduces the effects of stress on individuals and cuts down on absenteeism and turnover rates. From your point of view, the job will be a lot easier if staff are working with you, rather than against you.

This chapter looks at the characteristics of good teams and some of the ways you can help to build an effective team. It also considers the importance of morale and motivation.

## WHAT MAKES A SUCCESSFUL TEAM?

Being part of a winning team is an exhilarating experience — everyone works together to get results, and everyone benefits from the success. Even when things are not going well, there is help and support available from the rest of the team.

Good teams are made, not born. It takes hard work and effort to build a successful team, as you probably know from your own experience.

**Consider the teams that you did or do belong to. It could be sports, social, work — any kind of team. What makes them good teams? What are their characteristics? Write your responses in the space provided overleaf.**

**Below are some of the characteristics of successful teams. Which of the list of characteristics apply to your team?**

### Successful teams

☐   have a common goal;

☐   respect other team members;

☐   listen to one another;

☐   use all available talents;

☐   are well organised;

☐   have good leaders;

☐   work with one another, not against one another;

☐   are well motivated;

☐   have high standards;

☐   evaluate their effectiveness from time to time;

☐   contribute to the decision-making process;

☐   see conflict as a problem to be solved;

☐   see problems as challenges;

☐   have high morale;

☐   have regular team meetings;

give and take criticism;                                □

have a sense of humour;                                 □

are adaptable;                                          □

have a system of reward.                                □

As you can see, one of the keys to a successful team is a good team leader. Your role is crucial.

## LEADING THE TEAM

Women have not always been seen or, indeed, seen themselves as leaders. Leadership is not a traditional role for women. This can sometimes cause problems, either because female leaders are not taken seriously by colleagues, or because they do not have confidence in their own leadership abilities. Here are some of the main problems women managers themselves have identified:

- having a management style which is different from that of your predecessor;
- lack of suitable female role models;
- how to supervise men;
- jealousy and resentment of other women;
- how to delegate tasks to others;
- home/work conflict;
- trying to be 'nice' or popular;
- being the only female manager;
- being seen in a stereotyped role, eg as a daughter, mother, wife figure;
- comments that if a woman has a managerial position, this 'emasculates' her partner;
- feeling guilty;
- overcompensating for being a working woman (especially if there are children);
- how to give performance appraisal.

Why do women have specific problems in adopting a leadership role? As suggested earlier, part of the problem may stem from the fact that women are not brought up to see themselves as leaders. All this goes back to childhood socialisation. Studies indicate that the general skills acquired through team sports are crucial to effective leadership. And it is true to say that while team sports occupy an important role in a boy's life, for a girl they are relatively unimportant.

### What boys learn from games

- *Competing:* You have to win.
- *Cooperating*: You have to cooperate with others in order to win.
- *Tolerating*: It does not matter whether you like another boy or not. If he has 'winning talents', you need him for your team. Being liked is not as important as being a respected member of the team.
- *Working towards a common goal*: You must use the skills of all individuals.
- *Being part of a team:* You learn that to achieve individual success you need the support of a team. You develop a group identity which becomes more important than individual identity.
- *Leading and following*: You have to do both in order to survive.
- *Losing*: You are not devastated by failure — instead, you vow to do better next time.
- *Taking risks:* You do this in the interests of winning the game.
- *Planning and organising:* You plan every campaign meticulously, ensuring that everyone knows what is expected.
- *Accepting criticism*: You accept this from your leader and fellow team members in order to give your best performance for the team.
- *Interpreting rules*: You learn the rules; you challenge the rules; you bend the rules.
- *Accepting responsibility*: As team leader, you accept responsibility for failure — and share the recognition for any success.
- *Assessing and reacting*: You learn to assess strengths and weaknesses — your own and others' — in order to be successful.
- *Having stamina*: You need lots of energy to maintain your effectiveness.

- *Persevering*: You need the determination to succeed against all the odds.

Now, what about the girls? What do they get up to in the school yard?

When girls play together, they play in pairs or small groups. They tend to play games, such as skipping or hopscotch, which emphasise turn-taking, and in which there is not necessarily a winner. If a dispute arises, the relationship between individuals becomes more crucial than the outcome of the game. The 'process' is more important than the 'task'. For example, if girls start to squabble as they are playing a game, their solution usually is to change the game rather than to solve the conflict. Everything is subordinated to re-establishing harmony.

Girls set great store by friendships and find it difficult to play with someone whom they do not like. This kind of intimacy provokes jealousy, squabbling, and falling out.

As a result of all this, what do girls learn from their play?

## What girls learn from games

- *That they do not have to cope with losing*: It does not matter if you lose, because relationships are more important.
- *How to play games with no winners*: If you win, it means someone has to lose.
- *To avoid risks*: It is not worth taking chances, someone might get hurt.
- *To seek approval*: To be popular is all-important.
- *To avoid conflict*: Disputes must be avoided in order to maintain relationships.
- *To avoid decisions*: It is better to change the game than make a decision which might offend.
- *To be followers rather than leaders*: When boys and girls play together, notice who assumes the leadership role.

This is why at the age of 20, 30 or 40, many women have to learn the leadership skills that boys develop at the age of 10.

However, the good news is that management is a changing art. Many of the skills which are now considered important are those learned by girls at an early age. Skills such as cooperation, participation, and achieving consensus are now considered just as important in managing people as those learned by boys. This point is emphasised if you look at the ways to build an effective team.

## BUILDING THE TEAM

Here are some ways in which you can ensure that your team achieve their overall work objectives.

### Ten ways to build an effective team

1.  Create a common goal with objectives which can be reached only by team members cooperating with one another.

2.  Encourage team members to contribute towards the success of the team.

3.  Motivate and reward.

4.  Avoid favouritism and discrimination.

5.  Provide all necessary information and authority.

6.  Encourage open communication within the team.

7.  Organise team activities.

8.  Allow participation in the decision-making process.

9.  Be an appropriate role model.

10. Use the 'six most important words' when communicating with your team.

Now for some ways you can achieve this.

### Create a common goal

Success in most organisations depends upon people working together to achieve common goals. If you find that individuals are working against one another, do what you can to resolve the conflict, and to make your team aware of the negative effects this competition can have.

*Action points*

■ Identify the team goal and make certain everybody knows what it is and how they can achieve it together.
■ Do what you can to resolve any conflict that exists between team members. This may involve face-to-face counselling with one or two team members, rotating tasks, reviewing and re-allocating responsibilities, or even transferring somebody to another team.

**Encourage team members to contribute**

Every member of a team has a unique contribution to make towards success. As team leader, you have partial responsibility for the recognition and development of individual talents. Try to make sure that individuals do not become isolated. Encourage them to share their expertise and to evaluate one another's work.

*Action points*

■ Encourage people to learn from one another and share their expertise, by assigning tasks to a 'learner' and an 'expert' performer. This helps beginners to assimilate quickly.
■ Do not assume that just because people have always worked on particular jobs they are incapable of improvement. As you will be aware from what has been discussed already, women, in particular, often wait to be asked.
■ Rotate tasks, assignments and projects occasionally in order that individuals get an opportunity to show what they can do.

**Motivate and reward**

If you reward your staff in the right way, you will help to increase and sustain their motivation. These topics are dealt with fully later in this section.

**Avoid favouritism and discrimination**

Although it is natural that you should enjoy the company of some people more than others, as a manager, you are not wise to make your feelings apparent. Work should be allocated fairly, taking into account the talents, responsibilities and commitments of your team.

*Action points*

- Hold regular team meetings and briefing sessions.
- Meet your team members socially every so often, preferably not on an individual basis, but in small groups to avoid accusations of favouritism.
- Ask for suggestions for improving the way in which tasks are performed. The people who regularly carry out a particular task are often the last to be consulted when it comes to making changes.

**Provide all necessary information and authority**

When you allocate tasks to members of your team, make sure that you also give them all the information that they need to complete the job satisfactorily. This also applies to the authority to carry out the job, particularly when you are delegating new or important tasks. It is best not to set up a situation in which your staff have constantly to refer to you in order to do the job. This can frustrate them and stifle their initiative. Moreover, it wastes your time.

*Action points*

- Do not make your team members too dependent upon your expertise or approval.
- Give clear, unambiguous and full instructions.
- Reinforce what you say in writing, particularly if a task is new or complex.
- Make sure your staff know to whom they are accountable for a particular piece of work, and make certain they are accountable to one person only.
- Remember, as manager, you carry the ultimate responsibility — whether things go well or things go badly.

## Encourage open communication within the team

In this way, you will be able to spot problems at source, keep abreast of new ideas and information, and build rapport with your staff.

*Action points*

- Talk to your team and listen to what they say.
- Organise informal meetings.
- Set up a system of team briefings in order that each member knows what is happening within the organisation.

## Organise team activities

To build team spirit, you must encourage the team to work together on a daily basis. This not only encourages good individual relationships, but also introduces the concept of 'joint responsibility'.

*Action points*

- Hold weekly or monthly meetings.
- Hold brainstorming sessions to generate new ideas.
- If you have a large team, set up a 'team within a team' to tackle a particular task or project
- Set up working parties to find more effective ways of doing things.

## Allow participation in the decision-making process

People are most likely to accept and abide by any decisions that are made which affect them, if they have been consulted during the decision-making process. This does not mean that you are conceding your responsibility to make decisions to others. On the contrary, this is part of your role as a manager, and one which you will learn to approach with confidence and assertiveness. Consultation with your team in order to investigate their own ideas and perceptions on the problems you face will enable you to make the best decision — in everybody's interests.

*Action points*

- Consult the team before making a decision.
- Keep them informed of what is going on which concerns them.

## Be an appropriate role model

Be aware that the best way of teaching anybody anything is not by telling, but by example. The high expectations you have of your team will be totally undermined if you appear to disregard these standards when it comes to your own work and behaviour.

*Action points*

- Do what you say you will do.
- Never discuss one team member with another team member.

## Use 'the six most important words'

These words should be used constantly to express your appreciation of your team and your belief in the benefits of teamwork. The six most important words in the English language are:

> *I admit I made a mistake.*

The five most important words are:

> *You did a good job.*

The four most important words are:

> *What is your opinion?*

The three most important words are:

> *Let's work together.*

The two most important words are:

> *Thank you.*

The single most important word is:

> *We.*

You now have ten strategies to use in building an effective team, and here are some more suggestions from other women in situations similar to yours.

## Case studies

Anna Gilbert, Airport Duty Manager, Manchester Airport

I ensure that I'm highly visible and accessible and that people know what I do and respect me for it. It's important to have an interest in other people's jobs. For instance, it's no good saying, 'Is everything OK?' but not making the time to sit down and do something about it if it's not.

I also ensure that I'm well informed, particularly in my job, as I have encountered a lot of resistance because I'm a woman. People will tend to say, 'How can she know anything about my job?' If you are well informed, there's less chance of being caught out. On the shop-floor I'll tend to say, 'Show me your job', and ask what that person is doing and just observe them. That way you gain a real understanding of what your team are doing.

Christine Lyles, Equal Opportunities Manager, Barclays Bank, London

I have always found it's important to work *with* people. My style is to encourage people who work with me or for me to recognise what they want out of the job. It's no good my going home feeling pleased, with a sense of achievement, if others in the team don't feel the same way. Everyone should be aware of their own level of responsibility and be able to achieve personal satisfaction.

I used to have 30 staff working for me, so I broke the work down into sections and designated a team leader for each section. I found that way everyone was working to the overall goal and getting satisfaction from their own individual contribution.

**Now go back over the Action points and select at least three that you are going to implement at work.**

## How I will build an effective team

The third strategy you considered involved motivation and reward. In fact, these are perhaps the two most important elements in building and maintaining a successful team.

## MOTIVATION AND REWARD

All people work better when there is 'something in it' for them. This is what motivation means. But is money not enough? Is it not reasonable that people who are paid for doing a job should be expected to perform consistently well? Look round your own work environment, and you will agree that, yes, money does matter, but it is not the only motivator.

Most organisations operate on the principle that people serve to further the organisation's interests. But even some of the largest ones still do not recognise that their success will be enhanced if the individual's own interests are furthered at the same time. People have needs which drive them to act in particular ways. Here are some examples:

- friendship and love;
- recognition and esteem;
- development of personal potential;
- basic needs such as food, water and sleep;
- security — a steady job, a home, an income.

Human beings are continually striving to satisfy these needs. Satisfaction leads to survival, happiness, self-confidence and feelings of belonging. Thwarted needs lead to frustration, alienation, feelings of inferiority and poor motivation.

In looking at these needs, we must remember that they are not necessarily fulfilled at work. Many people achieve satisfaction for these needs outside work, in other activities. This is not to say that a manager should not attempt to satisfy these needs — but you are not the only one responsible for ensuring that these needs are met.

However, for most people, work is a large part of their lives, and it can provide the framework within which many of these needs are met. For many people, including those whose personal lives are filled with discord and problems, work may provide the greatest source of personal fulfilment. Motivating people is not always easy, particularly if you assume that what motivates you will also motivate them. This is not necessarily the case.

The following three steps make a good starting-point which can be applied to *all* staff.

### Three key steps to motivation

1. *Find out what your staff want.* They must want something — new skills, a promotion, satisfaction, etc. And they must want it strongly enough to be willing to do something about getting it. A person who has no goal or desire cannot be motivated.

2. *Establish how this need can be satisfied.* There must be some way in which the individuals you are responsible for can get what they want. It is no good wanting something, if there is no viable way of attaining it. A vital step in motivating individuals is to show them the path towards achieving what they want.

3. *Select a suitable reward.* People must know that their efforts, if successful, will be rewarded. Many individuals have goals and see ways of achieving them, but lack the faith that their hard work will be rewarded. People are not all the same in what they want and what they need; therefore, when you consider how to motivate your staff, you must treat each case on an individual basis.

## Motivating individuals

What can you do to motivate each member of your team? Here are some suggestions.

*Get to know your staff*

The three key steps outlined earlier all operate on the assumption that you make the necessary effort to get to know your staff. If you are new to a job, one of your first tasks should be to get to know the individual members of your team. The team will achieve the objectives that you set, but remember that this same team is made up of individuals of varying gender, age, ethnic origin, experiences and expectations.

Who are your staff? Make the effort to find out. Ask the right questions. How do they see their jobs? What aspirations do they have? What do they expect of you? What problems do they have at work? Do not sit in your office, pondering the answers to these questions. Observe your staff; talk to them; listen to what they have to say.

*Help them to achieve success*

As a manager, you will have to do your fair share of criticising performance, but if you find that this is what you are doing most of the time, there is something wrong. It is sometimes easier to criticise than to praise. Some managers tend to pass over the good things that people do, particularly if they have come to expect good work from subordinates, and then pounce upon any errors. This is a poor managerial tactic because people learn more from their successes than from their failures. Praise and encouragement go a long way towards achieving success.

*Give them a feeling of control over their lives*

Some managers exert a great deal of control over their staff because they do not trust them to take charge themselves. This attitude is counterproductive because it stifles initiative and creates unnecessary dependence upon the manager. People should feel that they are making some contribution

to the overall objectives of the team, section and organisation. They should be delegated work to match their
capabilities and experience.

### Build their self-esteem

Employees with high self-esteem work more effectively than
those with low self-esteem. It seems likely that people who
do not feel good about themselves probably do not care a
whole lot about work, either. It follows that, as a good manager, you should be doing what you can to build the self-
esteem of your staff.

It is easy to assume that mature people bring a healthy
degree of self-worth to the workplace with them. But what
the 'boss' says and does still carry a lot of weight. Therefore,
be liberal with your praise, and reinforce your staff as worthwhile and capable workers. You might tell them that they
did a good job, or that you enjoyed working with them on a
particular project. Being liberal with praise has fewer draw-
backs than withholding it.

Once you have motivated staff, you can then move on to
an appropriate reward.

## Rewards

How you recognise and reward success could considerably
affect your team's motivation. Here are some general guidelines.

### Use an appropriate reward

Here you need to know something about your staff. A
reward is motivating only if it is regarded as a reward by the
recipient. Use your knowledge of your staff to assess what
they judge to be appropriate rewards.

### Do not give everyone the same reward

Obviously, everyone has different needs and different interests. Remember that someone who has made substantial
progress should receive a greater reward than someone
who has made only token progress.

*Reward any effort made in the right direction*

If you are trying to motivate people to improve their performance, improvement is unlikely to happen overnight. In most cases you will be looking for a gradual change. Any signs for the better should therefore be recognised and rewarded, if only by a comment.

*Select what you reward*

If you are trying to change people's behaviour, you need to reward any sign that it is changing. If, however, you have specific expectations, rewarding people every time that they do improved work will soon lose its effect. A consequence of this might be that your staff come to depend on the reward in order to produce good work.

*Do not delay rewards*

Reward staff as soon as possible after the performance. A delayed reward will not have the desired effect.

*Ensure that staff know what they have to do to be rewarded*

This means that they have to have clear goals or objectives to start with as well as feedback on their performance. The feedback should answer the questions: 'Where did I go right or wrong?' and 'How should I move forward?'

*Make the reward fair and realistic*

Scale your rewards so that they are a true reflection of the performance being rewarded. Sometimes a word of praise will be all that is needed. Other times, a day off or a bonus might be more appropriate.

## Types of rewards

There are various ways in which you can reward your staff. What you do will depend upon the rewards that you are able to give, in your capacity as manager. Remember that the reward that you select should be seen as a reward by the person receiving it.

Tick the rewards you can give at present to staff you are responsible for at work. Then tick the ones that you would like to give.

| Possible rewards | Rewards I give | Rewards I would like to give |
| --- | :---: | :---: |
| Praise | ☐ | ☐ |
| Smile | ☐ | ☐ |
| Gratitude | ☐ | ☐ |
| Encouragement | ☐ | ☐ |
| Approval | ☐ | ☐ |
| Job security | ☐ | ☐ |
| Status symbol | ☐ | ☐ |
| Bonus/pay rise | ☐ | ☐ |
| Promotion | ☐ | ☐ |
| Time off | ☐ | ☐ |
| Challenging work assignments | ☐ | ☐ |
| A share in making decisions | ☐ | ☐ |
| More authority | ☐ | ☐ |
| Improved working conditions | ☐ | ☐ |
| Fun — parties, trips, drinks, etc | ☐ | ☐ |
| Prizes | ☐ | ☐ |
| More 'inside knowledge' | ☐ | ☐ |
| A move to a better team | ☐ | ☐ |
| A good performance appraisal | ☐ | ☐ |
| A recommendation in the 'right ear' | ☐ | ☐ |

Depending upon the job, the person, and the situation, all these things are good ways in which to reward effective performance. Some of these will be unrealistic because they are beyond your control; but some, such as recognition for a job well done, are within everyone's power to give. Do not underestimate the impact of a simple 'thank you'.

The following case study reveals what one manager has to say on the subject of motivation and reward.

## Case study

Christina Ezard, Branch Manager, Barclays Bank

I motivate my staff by making them feel part of a team. Participation is essential. The more I get my staff to do, the less pressure there is on myself, as I have my own targets to meet. I also leave my door open, so it's not seen as being 'me and them', but I do close it if I don't want any interruptions, and my staff respect that.

My staff have to contribute their own ideas. If I think their idea will work, I ask, 'How are you going to do it, and what assistance will you need?' They know I'm there if they need help. I believe in treating people well, giving them things to aim for and plenty of encouragement. If we need to reach a target at the end of the month it's no good saying, 'This month we have to achieve this', then leaving it and saying at the end of the month, 'Why haven't you done it?' So keep up to date with how things are going, and if everything is OK, tell them you know it is. If it's not, break it down into short-term goals which are easier to attain.

It's easy to give orders and for someone to react to that, but it doesn't develop that person or make them feel good about the work that they're doing. But if you involve them, look at their work, praise them if they do well, then they will respond. Often staff are only told how they're doing if they do something wrong. So my maxim is, 'Catch someone doing something right'.

**Write down at least three strategies from this section that you can use to motivate your staff.**

**How I can motivate my staff**

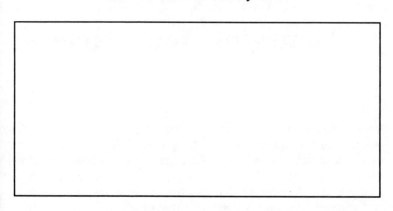

# 4
# Managing Your Time

Time and money are both precious commodities. However, most people can tell you how they spend their money; very few can say the same about their time. Time management is an important tool of your trade. Success in this area means that you use the time at your disposal to do what you consider to be important and achieve what you want.

Have you ever kept a time log? It involves writing down all your activities over a one- or two-week period. It is a good starting-point for improving your time management skills, as you can see exactly what you are doing — day in and day out. The results usually come as a bit of a shock, because rather than your spending time on important tasks, the week disappears beneath a mountain of routine matters and crises. This chapter is designed to help you manage your time. It looks at setting priorities (deciding what is important) and setting objectives (deciding how to achieve what is important). It also considers delegation and ways of minimising the impact of people and events which seem to consume so much of your day — everything from meetings to mail.

## SETTING PRIORITIES

How often do you hear yourself saying one or other of the following:

- If only I had more time.
- There ought to be more hours in the day.
- I wish I was better organised.
- I don't know where the time went.

It is difficult to manage your time effectively if you have no sense of what is important to you and what is urgent. You need to know both things in order to know what it is that you must do next. In other words, you need a sense of priority. Having a sense of priority is equally important outside as well as inside work.

## Personal priorities

If you want to get control of your time and your life, first ask yourself:

'*Who* and *What* are important in my life?'

**Now list your priorities both in and out of work and estimate how many hours you devote to each in an average week.**

| | Top ten personal priorities | Time spent |
|---|---|---|
| 1. | | |
| 2. | | |
| 3. | | |
| 4. | | |
| 5. | | |
| 6. | | |
| 7. | | |
| 8. | | |
| 9. | | |
| 10. | | |

What does your list include? Children, partner, work, religion, sports, friends, yourself? What is important is that there is a correlation between your priorities and the time spent on each. Are you spending enough time on your chosen priorities? If necessary, re-appraise them in the light of your findings. It is important for most people to have 'a balanced life'; that is, a life in which there is time and space for the things and people which are important to them.

Setting personal priorities, is essential to a career woman with a strong sense of personal objectives. The woman who can prioritise in her personal life will carry that ability into the workplace.

## Priorities at work

A manager cannot afford to spend time living from crisis to crisis. This way of working adversely affects performance, productivity, job satisfaction and, ultimately, health. However, as a manager, you are faced with the responsibility for achieving results, and this means that you have to work to deadlines. Therefore the use you make of your time is crucial. In situations such as crises, you will find that you have to make decisions under pressure. In order to cope, you have to have a system for defining what must be done, and in what order of priority to do it.

Start by asking yourself the following questions for each task which has to be done:

- Is the task important?
- Is the task urgent?

*Is the task important?*

An important task is something which will have a long-term effect, or something that is highly valued by the organisation.

*Is the task urgent?*

An urgent task is something which has to be done to meet a deadline. Urgent tasks can also be important, but this is not always the case. It is your responsibility to assess the importance and urgency of each task in the light of your own circumstances before coming to a decision. If you still find it difficult to determine what is important and urgent, ask yourself the following questions about a task:

- Does it have to be *now*?
- Does it have to be done by *me*?
- What will the consequences be if it doesn't get done?

Sometimes people do tasks in the order in which they were

given, without any thought as to which ones are important/ urgent and which ones can wait. A lot of tasks which take time are relatively trivial. People complete them first, in order to forget them, and by doing so, they neglect some of the more important ones. On other occasions people complete tasks they like and leave the unpleasant or difficult ones until last.

If you have problems setting your priorities, remember:

■ Top-priority tasks are those which are *both* important and urgent.
■ Medium-priority tasks are those which are *either* important or urgent.
■ Low-priority tasks are *neither* important or urgent.

It helps to define work priorities if you know what you are trying to achieve. In other words, what are your objectives?

## SETTING OBJECTIVES

You may refer to objectives as 'goals' or 'targets'. It does not matter what you call them; what matters is that you have them, and know how to identify them. They represent your commitment to action — now and in the future. It helps to plan your personal life if you have 'objectives' that you are working towards. You can then organise your time and your life more effectively.

The setting of objectives is even more crucial at work, as it is difficult to manage your time effectively if you are not clear about your goals. Your objectives will help to define your precise areas of responsibility, as well as to set targets for yourself. Achieving results through other people makes it essential that you have personal objectives and objectives for your staff. Without clear objectives, the success of work projects cannot be ensured.

Now, how do you go about setting objectives?

### How to set objectives

1. *Make your objective clear and unambiguous.* Unclear or

vague objectives can be misunderstood or misinterpreted by subordinates — and by yourself.

2. *Make your objective measurable or definable.* If you do not know when an objective has been reached, you cannot give reliable feedback or reward, either to yourself or your staff.

3. *Make your objective challenging but realistic.* You can motivate yourself and your staff with challenging objectives, but unrealistic objectives are discouraging.

4. *Make your objectives compatible with other objectives which have been set.* If objectives are not compatible, conflict and frustration will result.

5. *Make your objective performance-related.* When the objective contains an action word which is related to the performance expected, you and your staff will be in no doubt as to what you have to do to fulfil the objective.

**Here are some examples of work objectives. Add three of your own in the empty spaces.**

---

Work objectives

- To establish a department responsible for dealing with customer complaints and reducing complaint letters by 75 per cent by the end of the year.
- To make an effective presentation at the meeting to be held on 5 July, in order to persuade the committee to introduce the new process.
- To simplify the procedure for data collection from regional offices, in order to ensure that all data are available by the end of each month.

- 

- 

---

```



■




■



```

As a manager, you should have a clear understanding of the overall objectives for your work. If there is any doubt, go back to your job description and read it carefully. The overall objectives can then be broken down into subobjectives. For example, your overall objective might be to set up an effective performance appraisal system. From this main objective, you can derive several subobjectives. These might include:

■ To devise an evaluation system for each employee's role.
■ To draw up a staff information sheet outlining the benefits of performance appraisal.
■ To give the General Manager, Personnel, a regular update on each person's progress.
■ To arrange quarterly progress meetings with each member of staff.

**Now apply this exercise to your own job. Write down one, main, overall objective for your work at the moment and split it into at least three subobjectives.**

**Work objectives and subobjectives**

```
Main objective:



```

Subobjectives:

1.

2.

3.

4.

5.

Now check your objectives against this list to make sure that they are true objectives.

### Are my objectives true objectives?

☐     clear/unambiguous?

☐     measurable/definable?

☐     challenging/realistic?

☐     compatible with each other?

☐     performance-related?

If the answers are all 'yes', you have some specific objectives to work towards. If you answer 'no' to any of these questions, it may be useful for you to go back over this chapter again.

From this exercise you can see how your areas of responsibility become clearly defined for you. Practise setting objectives for yourself, and check to see that you are organising your time to meet these objectives. When you find that your time is being spent on other things, first re-examine your objectives to see if they are clear and achievable. Once you have learned to set your own objectives, you can then do the same thing for your team.

### Team objectives

When setting objectives, goals or targets for your team, try to remember these three basic guidelines:

1. *Consult* your team on the objectives to be set, rather than imposing objectives upon them. In this way, there is a much better chance that the objectives will be met.

2. *Agree* on realistic objectives.

3. *Set* objectives which encompass all the different aspects of the work involved.

Overleaf are some comments from other women managers on setting objectives.

Even if you prioritise and set clear objectives for your staff, you may still find yourself often overwhelmed with day-to-day problems and decisions related to your work. While it is true that you carry the overall responsibility for the work of your team, it is quite inappropriate to do all the work, or to take all the decisions yourself. Some responsibilities and some decisions could and should be delegated to members of your team.

## DELEGATION

Some managers delegate readily, while others may do so reluctantly. There can be many reasons for this reluctance. Some managers believe they can do things more quickly themselves, and, in the short term, this may be true. However, it is false economy, as time spent now training a member of staff will relieve you of the task for good. It means you get rid of a routine matter, to concentrate on more important things. The individual, in turn, is better motivated through being given additional responsibility. Also, if you train staff well, set standards, and monitor progress, mistakes will be minimised.

Some managers feel 'in control' if doing everything themselves. In fact, they are the ones with least control. In some cases, they spend their whole time carrying out routine tasks of no relevance to their career development. In other cases, they spend their time moving from crisis to crisis because they have never taken the time to train anyone else how to do a particular task.

## Case studies

Marilyn Day, Senior Nursing Manager, Community Psychiatric Nursing Services, Coventry

> I believe that it's important that we don't just do our jobs, but that we meet the objectives of local management and the service as a whole. I've drawn up a plan to meet each of my team for around an hour each month, to discuss cases and address broader issues. It's not a personal performance review, but a means of dealing with general matters which must be addressed if our objectives are to be met. One outcome might be that training needs are identified. It's my staff who own and implement operational policies — they review practices and offer alternatives to improve the way they work. Most importantly, ideas need to be clearly communicated. Time must be given for them to be duly considered, and if they improve the means by which our objectives will be met, their implementation should be fully supported.

Equal Opportunities Manager, Local County Council

> I believe in giving people information. If people are more informed and realise where they fit into an organisation, they're more likely to see the direction in which they should be going in terms of aims and objectives.
>
> If you set objectives and they need adjusting, admit the mistakes you have made and perhaps ask someone else how they would do this job. I also try to plan each week in advance, but, as many deadlines are already laid down, if something urgent crops up, plans sometimes go awry.

Some managers believe their staff are not capable, and never give them the opportunity to demonstrate what they can do. If staff do not have the opportunity to prove themselves, they tend to withdraw into the background — or withdraw to another company which does recognise their potential. Most staff are pleased to have work delegated to them as long as it is not regarded as 'off-loading' from you. Delegate interesting as well as routine tasks — do not keep all the best for yourself.

Some managers feel insecure, so insecure that they fear that if others can perform delegated tasks with ease, their own position is undermined. The point is that managers are judged on the results of the team as a whole. If the team performs well, the glory is reflected on the manager as leader of that team. Also, feelings of insecurity are soon evident to other staff, and there are people who will swing the situation to their advantage — and play on the apparent weakness.

If you, as a manager, are not to be totally overwhelmed by work, and all its attendant stresses and strains, you *must* delegate. There are good reasons to do so.

## Delegation — who benefits?

The benefits of skilful delegation will be gained by you, your organisation and your team.

*You* will benefit by delegating some of your tasks to others and thereby having more time to plan, organise and coordinate the work of the department. Delegation will enable you to handle other matters which may be in need of more specialist attention than the members of your team can provide. You may be able to develop yourself by taking on more advanced work. It is important that you, as a manager, allow yourself 'thinking time' when you have no work scheduled. This becomes more crucial the higher up the management ladder you go. 'Thinking time' is not 'wasted time'. It enables you to use your creative powers to solve problems, to come up with innovative ideas, and to take a wider view of things. Delegating will give you more time in which to do this.

*Your organisation* will benefit and departmental efficiency should be improved by enabling decisions to be made at the lowest possible staff level. Greater employee involvement in decision-making is likely to reap dividends in terms of increased motivation and improved work performance. Delegation also develops managerial potential in employees which the organisation may be able to draw on later. Finally, crises caused by absences or promotion may be avoided if there are other people available to take over some of the managerial tasks.

*Your team* will benefit, and those to whom work is delegated will be able to increase their competence and skills as a result of what they do. This may increase their commitment and overall job satisfaction, particularly if satisfactory completion of the work is linked to a system of approval and rewards. Receiving delegated work encourages team members to use their initiative. Their motivation and morale are increased, and they have an opportunity to demonstrate potential and perhaps unused talents. Their personal development is enhanced alongside their career development. The importance of this cannot be overestimated.

The process involved in delegation answers the following questions:

- What should I delegate?
- To whom should I delegate?
- How should I delegate?

**What should I delegate?**

There are six types of work which can be delegated to members of your team.

### Types of work to delegate

1.  Minor routine work — particularly work which has to be covered whether you are absent or present. Some of these tasks may be time-consuming and yet not need your level of competence.

2.  Work which will help to test and develop team members — a range of interesting and increasingly complex tasks which will challenge your staff and increase their competence.

3.  Work which requires expert or specialist attention — this may be work that you can do particularly well, and thus you can pass on your expertise.

4.  Work which a team member can do as well as a mana-

ger — look at tasks where a team member's skills and experience will be particularly valuable.

5. Work which you may be less qualified to do — just because you are the manager does not mean that you are necessarily the best at everything.

6. New work — procedures brought about by departmental or organisational changes which would be time-consuming for you to undertake.

Not all your work can be delegated. Certain types of work should *not* be delegated.

### Types of work not to delegate

1. Crises.

2. Specific personal matters and confidential matters.

3. Policy making.

## To whom should I delegate?

### Delegate to:

■ people who are directly responsible to you;
■ people who have potential, those who need more responsibility, those who need a challenge, and those who may feel frustrated by lack of promotional opportunity;
■ people who have weaknesses in areas which can be helped by your experience;
■ people whose development will contribute to the success of the individual, the team, yourself, and the organisation;
■ the lowest level at which the job can be done. But remember, if you bypass an immediate subordinate to delegate work lower down the line, inform the subordinate why you have chosen someone else to do this work.

## How should I delegate?

Before you delegate, the task must be clearly defined in your own mind. When you call in a member of your staff to assign a job, use the following ten steps to ensure you delegate effectively.

own mind. When you call in a member of your staff to assign a job, use the following ten steps to ensure you delegate effectively.

### Step-by-step delegation

1. Describe the assignment — the overall goal.

2. Set objectives — the specific tasks.

3. Indicate performance standards — how staff will know the task has been carried out to your satisfaction.

4. Allow questions — throughout your instructions.

5. Check understanding — regularly.

6. Indicate responsibility — who is in control?

7. Give some useful examples — to illustrate your points.

8. Indicate review and follow-up procedure — in order that a check on performance standards can be made.

9. Provide all the necessary resources, and ensure that everything needed to complete the task is provided.

10. Provide the necessary authority — will any decisions need to be made in your absence? Clear the lines of access to information. Indicate to all involved that the authority has been given.

**Write down five activities which you perform on a regular basis, which could be delegated to members of your team.**

### My tasks

**Now choose *one* of these activities to delegate to someone else within the next two weeks.**

Describe the work to be delegated:

Why do you want to delegate this particular task?

What will you gain from delegating it?

Who in your team has the time, knowledge, skill and motivation to perform the task?

What will this person gain from doing the task?

When will you delegate this task?

```
┌─────────────────────────────────────────────────┐
│                                                 │
│                                                 │
│                                                 │
└─────────────────────────────────────────────────┘
```

All that remains for you to do is to delegate effectively by following the ten steps. Use the following check-list whenever you have a task to delegate.

### Check-list for effective delegation

- ☐ Describe the assignment.
- ☐ Set objectives.
- ☐ Indicate performance standards.
- ☐ Allow questions.
- ☐ Check understanding.
- ☐ Indicate responsibility.
- ☐ Give some useful examples.
- ☐ Indicate review and follow-up.
- ☐ Provide all the necessary resources.
- ☐ Provide the necessary authority.

Remember that once you have delegated a task, you should not interfere. It is very easy to discourage staff by constantly checking on what they are doing. The balance may be hard to find at first, but the more you delegate, the more confident your staff will become at tackling new projects. And the less you have to check on what they are doing, the more time you will have for doing other things.

Finally, let us look at how to control some of the things that seem to rob you of time.

### TIME ROBBERS

Things happen every day at work which stop you from achieving your objectives. Your work is interrupted by staff, or a sudden request causes you to drop everything you intended to do that day. Meetings are a regular part of the job of a manager, as is the interminable mountain of paperwork. Also, when an emergency or crisis occurs, the manager must deal with it. None of these events waste your time. Instead, they consume your time — leaving you with the feeling, where did the day go?

How can you minimise the impact of such events?

## Interruptions

> 'If I get one more interruption, I'll scream'.

How many times do you start to do something, only to have your concentration disturbed by a telephone call, a knock at the door, or an unexpected visitor? Although the interruptions may not be long, they can take their toll in disturbed concentration if your time is constantly fragmented in this way.

Women are often more accustomed than are men to being constantly available when needed, and it takes a strong will to adopt a different strategy sometimes.

It is not possible — or advisable — to eliminate all interruptions, as some of them may turn out to be priorities. Indeed, it is true to say that an interruption is often a priority for the interrupter. But you have to find a way of minimising the disruption of your work and concentration if you are going to make the best use of your time. Here are three suggestions.

*Set aside periods when you are not to be disturbed*

Easier said than done, you might think, but it is possible. If your staff know that you are not available to them or anybody else during a particular time of the day, you should have a period when you can get on without interruptions. Arrange for your assistant to take telephone calls and deal with any other enquiries. Make sure that these are all entered on a log in order that you can see at a glance what happened when you were unavailable.

Having set up a system such as this, stick to it. It is no use expending time and energy in explaining that you are not to be disturbed, only to keep popping out to find out how everyone is coping, or to allow someone to interrupt you 'just this once'.

### Allow times for specific activities

Here are some examples of activities that you could schedule for specific times of the day or week:

- telephone calls;
- paperwork;
- meetings with team members;
- meeting external suppliers;
- research/reading;
- report writing.

If you are busy and unavailable for much of the working week, you could set up a time when your staff know that you are available, and that their interruptions will receive your undivided attention. An 'open door' policy is not for the whole week, but being accessible for at least some of the time is something that a manager should regard as important for good staff relations.

### Be firm but polite

No matter how good a system you have for getting on with your work in an uninterrupted fashion, you will always have to contend with the person who demands: 'Have a minute?' The alternatives in this situation are:

- You lose your temper and offend the unexpected caller. Later, you feel guilty for having reacted in that way.
- You agree to see the person and feel furious with yourself afterwards for not being more assertive.
- And the best way: you tell callers firmly but politely that you are busy at present and arrange to see them at a mutually convenient time.

  'I'm really busy at the moment; how about popping in for a minute at lunchtime?'

or

'I'm really pressed for time right now; can we fix a time to
meet later?'

Choosing the third alternative means that you maintain
your relationship with the other person, while at the same
time ensuring that your time is respected.

## Requests and invitations

Requests and invitations often come in the form of interruptions, and if you are pressed for time, it is a frequent, but
foolish, response to agree in order to get rid of the other person — you then repent at leisure. You cannot do everything
that you are asked, and you have to accept this. Not all
requests are reasonable, and there may be some which are
simply undesirable. Yet people often believe that they do
not have the right to refuse, agree in order to please, and feel
annoyed later for having done so.

Women, in particular, find it very difficult to refuse
requests. This is partly through being brought up to put
other people's needs first, but also because they worry about
the impact that a refusal will have upon other people, and
the relationship with them. Will they be angry? This is a difficult reaction to cope with, for many women; therefore they
agree and do what they do not want to do.

The best strategies to adopt when faced with a trouble-
some request or invitation are to delay the decision and to
learn to say 'No'.

### *Delay your decision*

It is never a good idea to answer on the spur of the moment.
If you receive an unexpected request or invitation, it is quite
reasonable for you to be allowed some time in which to
make up your mind. For example, you could reply, 'Thank
you for asking. I can't give you an answer at present, but I
will let you know tomorrow.' In this way, you allow yourself
more time in which to make a decision that you are happy
with. Then, you need to ask yourself if you really want to
agree, and perhaps consider what the consequences of
refusing might be.

*Learn to say 'No'*

If you are still not sure how to do this, have a look at Chapter 1 again. If you do say 'No' in an assertive and direct way, people are unlikely to persist, unless they are a real nuisance. If they do, repeat what you have said, calmly and firmly, as many times as is necessary for them to get the message. This technique if often called 'the broken record', because that is what you sound like until your point is driven home.

## Meetings

Meetings can be a great time-waster at work because, as someone once said, 'When all is said and done, there is far more said than done.' However, attending meetings is an aspect of your role that you will be quite familiar with as a manager, particularly as a female manager, because of the importance of being visible and making your point of view known. This does not mean that you have to waste time, as it makes sense to attend only the ones where your presence is absolutely necessary.

There are a few questions to ask yourself before you decide to attend the next meeting.

- Is this meeting really necessary?
- Could the agenda be dealt with in some other way, eg by letter, telephone or individual communication?
- Do I have the right to refuse to attend? If you do not, then the decision has been made for you.
- Does it have to be me that attends? Ask yourself if someone else could go in your place, in order for your time to be spent more productively.

If you have answered all these questions and concluded that you still have to attend, you can minimise the impact by using the following check-list:

### Meeting check-list

- **Check** that there is an objective for the meeting.
- **Check** that there is an agenda.

- **Check** that there is a precise finishing time.
- **Check** that you are well prepared.
- **Check** that you know what you want out of the meeting.
- **Check** that actions and tasks are assigned.
- **Check** that your contribution was worthwhile and effective.

**Paperwork**

Paperwork is a routine task that all managers have to contend with, and the standard advice is to handle each piece of paper once only. This means that you do one of the following:

- read it and take action;
- read it and file it;
- read it and bin it.

What you should not do is add it to an already overflowing in-tray.

Another way of relieving the tedium of paperwork is to train yourself to read more efficiently. This means curbing any tendency to read every word of an article or report, and concentrating on the key ideas. Read only the details that are relevant to your purpose, and highlight the interesting bits for future reference.

**Crises**

Many crises can be avoided by planning. However, 'even the best-laid plans . . .' In the event of a crisis, it may help if you bear the following guidelines in mind:

*Anticipate problems*

Many problems can be avoided by careful planning. Try to envisage as far as possible what might go wrong. You could prevent a problem from arising in the first place.

*Consider the situation carefully*

In a crisis, when the adrenalin is flowing, the mind often

seems to go blank. This is not the best frame of mind in which to make rational decisions; thus, it helps if you can pause for a moment and take stock of the situation.

### Seek help, if necessary

Do not assume that you have to cope alone, even if the crisis has come about because of something you did — or did not do. You will probably need support; do not be afraid to ask for it. It is in everybody's interests for crises to be managed as quickly and as painlessly as possible; ask yourself who can offer the best support — then ask for it.

### Tell people what is going on

When you have a crisis to contend with, it often has repercussions on other areas, and there is nothing so frustrating from other people's point of view as suspecting that something is wrong, yet not knowing what it is. Let those you are working with know what is going on. You do not need to go into great detail about the problem if you do not want to. But it helps to keep people informed of any major crises, in order that they can understand any sudden changes which might affect them.

### Take appropriate action then evaluate how well you coped

Ask yourself if your strategies for coping worked. If not, what would have helped? What would you do differently next time? Try to discover what you have learned from this crisis which could help to avoid — or minimise the impact — next time.

The ability to cope in a crisis is one of the hallmarks of a good manager, and the guidelines hold true for crises which may happen at work or at home. The important thing is to weather the storm, with as little stress to yourself as possible. You will need all your resources to deal with problems such as these, and a panic reaction to such a situation will only drain your energies and leave you too fraught to cope.

This is what some other women managers have to say on the subject of crises.

## Case studies

**Ann Webster, Equal Opportunities Officer, Derby City Council**

Everything was in hand for our usual monthly Equal Opportunities Awareness course. The candidates had all been invited; the course programme finalised; room and refreshments booked. You could say this was 'the calm before the storm', because just a few days before the course, my co-presenter was suddenly taken ill.

After the panic bells had stopped ringing, I thought about the situation I was in. Rather than cancel the course, I decided to go ahead, even though I was unfamiliar with my co-presenter's material. To overcome this, I changed the whole structure of the course, using a new Equal Opportunities Training Guide I'd received a few days earlier. On the day I nearly lost my nerve, but went ahead with the day-long course. I was dreading feedback, as I'd taken a risk in changing a course that had been running for several years. However, I need not have worried. I am still on cloud nine from all the praise and compliments I received. If I'd chickened out at the last minute, I would not have had that wonderful feeling of turning a crisis into a successful venture.

**Jill Murkin, Training Manager, Marks and Spencer, London**

My department is responsible for sending out training material to stores within set deadlines. We recently had a situation when food legislation changed and we were faced with a major communication problem. It was decided that the necessary training information had to be sent out for communication to all food staff within a week, so that they could be trained in the new procedures.

It is important when faced with this type of situation not to panic; invariably there is a way around problems. If a member of my team is involved, we sit down and decide how we are going to tackle it.

I'm a practical person, so I tend not to think in terms of crises, but rather see problems in the light of solutions — then decide what is the best and quickest way to get out of them. It's also important to think positively in this type of situation.

With regard to the 'food problem', we revised and reprinted a section of the relevant guide, helped to draft a letter which managers would find acceptable, and produced a poster highlighting the changes — all within two weeks.

Now move on to complete your action plan.

# Action Plan

Now it is time to draw up your personal action plan — things you are going to start doing — or stop doing — to improve your effectiveness as a manager. To help your formulate your plan, you may like to refer to the exercises you have completed throughout this book. You may like to look back at:

- ten good reasons to be assertive;
- the rights you would like to have;
- the three-line strategy for stating what you want to happen;
- the six steps to effective communication;
- your completed communication chart;
- eight steps for giving instructions;
- check-list on non-verbal communication;
- the rewards you can and cannot give;
- your personal priorities;
- the exercise on delegation;
- how to deal with time robbers.

Here is an extract from one woman's action plan:

| Things I am going to start/stop doing | Made a start | Getting there | Doing well |
|---|---|---|---|
| 1. Stop apologising every time I say no. | ✔ 22 Feb | ✔ 1 March | |
| 2. Complete paper-work first thing every morning. | ✔ 12 Feb | | |
| 3. Delegate time sheet analysis to Dianne. | ✔ 12 Feb | ✔ 19 Feb | ✔ 26 Feb |

The following list shows how to write your own action plan.

### How to write an action plan — step by step

1.  Select *three* things you are going to start or stop doing as a manager. You might like to begin with something relatively easy to boost your confidence.

2.  Write them down the left-hand column.

3.  Come back to the list in a week and review progress.

4.  When you have achieved what you resolved to do, tick the column and date it.

5.  When you have achieved your goal on three occasions or have completed the task you set yourself, you are entitled to feel pleased with your progress. You have achieved what you set out to do.

6.  As you complete one task, add others to the bottom of the list — an action plan is an ongoing process.

The secret is — do not work on too many tasks at one time. Take things a step at a time and progress to more difficult areas, later rather than sooner.

| Things I am going to start/stop doing | Made a start | Getting there | Doing well |
|---|---|---|---|
| | | | |

| Things I am going to start/stop doing | Made a start | Getting there | Doing well |
|---|---|---|---|
| | | | |

If you find that the strategy is effective, it will probably become part of your normal pattern of work or behaviour within a short time.

If you find that something does not work immediately, do not give up. You cannot change long-standing habits overnight. Continue your efforts to find techniques that work for *you*. Speak to other women about what they do to relieve your particular problem. Most of them will be only too willing to help, if asked.

Remember, also, that some of the changes you decide to make may not always be appreciated by others, especially in the early days. The things which make your burden lighter are not always in the interests of other people. It may suit them better if you do not change. Be aware that time may be needed for readjustment, as people may feel unsettled, even threatened, by any changes you make.

The best advice is to communicate. Let people know how you feel; listen to their point of view, without being critical or judgemental. By doing this, you have the best chance of achieving cooperation and support.

Good luck and good managing!

# Further Reading

Alkenson, Jacqueline (1988) *Coping with Stress at Work*, Thorsons, Wellingborough.

Armstrong, Michael (1990) *How to be an Even Better Manager*, Kogan Page, London.

Bryce, Lee (1989) *The Influential Woman*, Piatkus, London.

Chambers, C, Cooper, S and McLean, A (1990) *Develop Your Management Potential*, Kogan Page, London.

Chapman, Elwood (1988) *How to Develop a Positive Attitude*, Kogan Page, London.

Cooper, Cary and Davidson, Marilyn (1984) *Women in Management*, Heinemann, London.

——and Lewis, S (1989) *Career Couples*, Unwin, London.

Courtis, John (1988) *44 Most Common Management Mistakes*, Kogan Page, London.

Crabtree, Stan (1991) *Moving Up*, Kogan Page, London.

Davidson, Marylin (1985) *Reach for the Top*, Piatkus, London.

Dickson, Ann (1985) *A Woman in Your Own Right*, Quartet, London.

Dyer, Wayne (1985) *Pulling Your Own Strings*, Hamlyn, Twickenham.

——(1986) *Your Erroneous Zone*, Sphere, London.

Ernst & Young (1991) *The Manager's Self-Assessment Kit*, Kogan Page, London.

Evans, R and Russell, P (1989) *The Creative Manager*, Unwin, London.

Fisher, Roger and Ury, William (1986) *Getting to Yes*, Hitchinson, London.

Haddock, Patricia and Manning, Marylyn (1989) *Leadership Skills for Women*, Kogan Page, London.

Hansard Society Commission (1990) *Women at the Top*, Hansard Society, London.

Haynes, Marion (1988) *Effective Meeting Skills*, Kogan Page, London.

Lindley, Patricia and Makin, Peter (1991) *Positive Stress Management*, Kogan Page, London.

Lloyd, Sam (1988) *How to Develop Assertiveness*, Kogan Page, London.

McDonald, Janet (1986) *Climbing the Ladder*, Methuen, London.

Minzberg, Henry (1973) *The Nature of Managerial Work*, Harper and Row, New York.

Moates-Kennedy, Marilyn (1984) *Powerbase: How to Build It, How to Keep It*, Fawcett Crest, Wetherby.

Morris, M J (1988) *First Time Manager*, Kogan Page, London.

National Economic Development Office (NEDO) (1990) *Women Managers* Kogan Page, London.

Paul, Nancy (1984) *The Right to be You*, Chartwell Bratt, Bromley.

Powell, G N (1988) *Women and Men in Management*, Sage, London.

Rhodes, J and Thame, S (1988) *The Colours of Your Mind*, Fontana, London.

Shaevitz, Marjorie (1984) *The Superwoman Syndrome*, Fontana, London.

Siewart, Lothar (1989) *Managing Your Time*, Kogan Page, London.

Skinner, Jane and Fritchie, Rennie (1988) *Working Choices*, J M Dent, London.

Spenser, L and Young, K (1990) *Women Managers in Local Government: Removing the Barriers*, LGMB, London.

Women Returners' Network (1991) *Returning to Work*, Kogan Page, London.

# Further Information

Business in the Community
227A City Road
London EC1
Tel: 071-253 3716

Confederation of British
  Industry
Centre Point
103 New Oxford Street
London WC1A 1DU
Tel: 071-379 7400

Domino Consultancy Ltd
56 Charnwood Road
Shepshed
Leicestershire LE12 9NP
Tel: 0509 505404

European Women's
  Management
  Development Network
EWMD Secretariat
c/o EFMD
40 Rue Washington
B-1050 Brussels
Belgium
UK Secretary: Christine
  Barham
Tel: 0442 843491

Equal Opportunities
  Commission
Overseas House
Quay Street
Manchester M3 3HN
Tel: 061-833 9244

Industrial Society:
  Pepperell Unit
Robert Hyde House
48 Bryanston Square
London W1H 7LN
Tel: 071-262 2401

Trade Union Congress
Great Russell Street
London WC1
Tel: 071-636 4030

United Kingdom Federation
  of Business and
  Professional Women
23 Ansdell Street
London W8 5BN
Tel: 071-938 1729

Women in Management
64 Marryat Road
Wimbledon
London SW19 5BN
Tel: 081-944 6332